BUILDING A SUCCESSFUL FAMILY

Basic Building Blocks For A Healthy Home

DR. JERRY PIPES

Other Related Books Available:

Family to Family
by Dr. Jerry Pipes and Victor Lee

Becoming Complete
by Dr. Jerry Pipes
New edition will be released in 2004

Printed in the United States of America.

ISBN 0-9719068-0-7 9.99

TABLE OF CONTENTS

Introduction   **Page**
     Portrait of an American Family

Section One: **Getting Started on the Biggest Investment**
     You'll Make!
 Chapter I.   The Blueprint of a Successful Family   5

Section Two: **Building Your Successful Home**
 Chapter II.   Laying Your Foundation—Success is an Inside Job! 17
 Chapter III.   Building the Walls—A Healthy Marriage   23
 Chapter IV.   Roofing for Maximum Protection—Self-Esteem   41
 Chapter V.   Wiring for Sound—Communication   55

Section Three: **Maintain and Increase the Value of**
     Your Investment
 Chapter VI.   Adding Insulation—Mentoring Your Children   65
 Chapter VII. Purchasing a Warranty—Building Internal Fences   79

Section Four: **Rebuilding from the Storms, Neglect,**
     or Other Disasters
 Chapter VIII. Protecting Your Home—Moving Through
     the Tough Times   95

Section Five: **Protecting Your Investment**
 Chapter IX.   Insuring Your Home—Developing a Successful
     Worldview   105

Introduction

It has been twelve days since Mom, Dad, Eric, Janey, and Melissa Morgan had a meal together.

No, Dad is not out of town, and no one is angry. They did not plan it this way, but they figure that's just the way life is today.

You see, Eric's bus leaves for high school at 7:05 a.m. Janey leaves for middle school at 7:40 a.m. Mom takes Melissa to elementary school at 8:45 a.m., then she's off to work. She works three-quarters time so she can be with the children–in reality, the only time she is "with" the children–is in the van. She feels more like a taxi driver than a "mom."

Janey, one of the top acrobatic and jazz dancers in her troop, has advanced dance class after school on Monday, Tuesday, and Thursday until 6:00 p.m. (with an occasional Saturday morning rehearsal thrown in).

Eric's high school basketball team, off to a 2-7 start, is practicing overtime every day after school, except on days when there are games.

Melissa wants to be a dancer like Janey, so she practices with the beginner group as soon as Janey's class is over.

THIS FAMILY HAS FALLEN VICTIM
TO THE AMERICAN CULTURE

Monday night is basketball practice. Monday, Tuesday, and Thursday night is dance. Almost every Friday or Saturday night, at least one of the children is spending the night with a friend. And Saturday is lawn day, basketball game day, dance performance day–the list is endless.

Mom is taking a computer course on Tuesday evenings. Some of Dad's clients insist on dinner meetings; there seems to be two or three per week.

> *Perhaps you recognize this family.*

Stretched, stressed, and losing touch with each other, this family is easy to find. They live in your neighborhood, on your block–maybe in your house. Whether you are raising your children with your spouse, are a single parent, or have not begun a family yet, you do not want to live like the Morgans.

This family has fallen victim to the American culture. American Family Association research shows:

◆ Only thirty-four percent of America's families eat one meal together each day.

◆ The average father spends only eight to ten minutes a day with the children–including television and meals.

◆ Only twelve percent of America's families pray together.

◆ The average couple spends only four minutes of uninterrupted time together a day.

Renowned researcher George Barna writes, "The statistics also point out that although most adults regard family as their most satisfying aspect of life, they also regard it as their most frustrating. Believe me, we have a family crisis in America today."

But why? Is there anything wrong with the above family's activities? The children's athletic activities are healthy, aren't they? They teach discipline, commitment, and how to win and lose. Dad has to do business, doesn't he? And Mom, after shuttling the children to and from school and looking after them all these years, has the right to take a class so she can refine her own interests, doesn't she?

The truth is that there is nothing wrong with any particular element of the above family's schedule. But collectively, they add up to a family who knows what each other does, but does not know each other. They are a mom and dad who provide physically, but do not make the time to provide emotionally. Each of the above family members is searching for significance–Eric through basketball; Janey through dance; Melissa through trying to be like Janey; Mom through serving and caring for her children; and Dad through providing financially. In the midst of it all, they have lost the significance of what they were designed to be–a family. Their efforts are individual and misdirected rather than unified and focused as a family.

This all-too-typical family is like a pressure cooker. The instructions for operating a pressure cooker might look something like this:

1. Check pressure regulator vent, pressure indicator stem, and safety tubes before opening.
2. For best results fill one-half to two-thirds full. DO NOT OVER-FILL!
3. Indicator stem rises when cooker is under pressure.
4. When fully pressurized, regulator will "hiss and rock." This is normal and allows excessive steam to escape.

Is your family hissing and rocking? Is it overfilled? Do you have a clue what the pressure indicators are? If mishandled, a pressure cooker will explode. If mishandled, so will your family!

This brief excerpt from my book, *Family to Family*, illustrates perfectly that stress and time pressures are the greatest enemy of the American family. *Building a Successful Family* will help you avoid an explosion in your family. This will happen as you discover a sense of purpose as a family, develop core values, and then prioritize around them. The result will be more quality and quantity time with your family. You will learn how to bring the fun back into your marriage, build bridges of communication, establish identity and self-esteem in your children, and how to take the frustration out of the discipline process.

The principles in this volume have been born out of the oven of over twenty-seven years of study and working with parents and students. While completing my studies at the bachelor's, master's, and doctoral levels, I took every opportunity to deepen my understanding of psychology, sociology, marriage, and family. In the years since, I have averaged reading thirty-six books a year again focusing primarily on personal growth and family issues. Not all of the illustrations in this book originated with me, nor do I remember where I first read or heard of some of them. I am indebted to the writers, speakers, and researchers who have stretched, shaped, and helped me form the principles shared in these pages. At the end of Chapters Two through Nine, you will find a limited number of Additional Suggested Resources that reflect the best of the best from my reading. These resources will strengthen your personal and family life as they have mine. Further, this volume has not been written from an academic frame of reference. I have intentionally made this book informal and conversational in order to facilitate a warm dialogue with you, the reader.

The *Building a Successful Family Conference* has been shared with hundreds of thousands of people around the world. Though I have had the incredible privilege of standing in front of a lot of people, please know that I don't understand all the questions–much less have all the answers. These pages will reflect what I like to call "helpful hints from a fellow struggler."

I am grateful to Robert Vickers for the end of chapter activities and ideas. They are awesome! You will find them so helpful. Bob's tireless work and suggestions have been invaluable in preparing this manuscript. I would like to thank Dr. Tal Davis, Dr. Ron Mumbower, Debbie Pipes, Dr. Brian Waite, and Lyn Waldron for their suggestions–they were more help than they will ever know. Also, I am thankful to Debra, Paige, and Josh for allowing me to share a few of our family events in order to add value to others. Finally, I appreciate the students, parents, and business leaders who have allowed their stories to be included. While no names are mentioned, these events bring the principles of this book to life.

The road to a successful family will not be easy. *Building a Successful Family* is not a quick fix, but rather the beginning of a rewarding life-long journey that will help any family get off the activity-driven merry-go-round and on to genuine family health. Congratulations on choosing to Build a Successful Family!

Dr. Jerry Pipes

Section One

Getting Started on the Biggest Investment You'll Ever Make

> **I have been very happy with my homes, but homes really are no more than the people who live in them. —Nancy Reagan**

Chapter I.
The Blueprint of a Successful Family

Have you ever been to a T-ball game? That's where young children are not even old enough to hit a moving object, so they hit a little ball sitting on top of a tee. Use your imagination. A little guy steps up to bat, he is as big as you can be and play T-ball. He's got the big league chew, bubble gum, of course. He pulls the bat back and literally swings as hard as he can. He almost misses the ball, but instead, barely taps it, and as a result, it literally dribbles to the short stop (He is as young and small as you can be and play T-ball) who bends over and scoops up the ball. It's the first time in his life that he catches a moving object in a game–he is so excited that he pulls the ball to his chest and smiles.

Now, of course, the problem with this picture is that the guy who hit the ball is running to first. The guy who was on first is running to second, the guy who was on second is running to third and the pitcher who was playing that position defensively says, "Throw the ball to third!" As the shortstop pulls it to his chest and smiles–he's so proud he caught it–the rest of the infield gets into it along with the outfield and everybody is yelling together, "Throw the ball to third!" And the coach–coaches in Little League amaze me, because they never get emotionally involved, right? We have the coach with both hands and both feet on the chain link fence dugout pulling the entire dugout back and forth screaming with the rest of the team, "Throw the ball to third!" At this point the kid is getting frustrated. He knows something else needs to be done; by now even the opposing parents are pulling for this kid. Everyone in the ballpark is yelling together, "Throw the ball to third!" The kid, at the peak of his frustration, screams out, "Momma, where's third?"

Where's third?

There are a lot of students in America who are screaming out today to anyone who will listen, "Where is third?"

Every year, more than 1,100,000 middle-school and high-school girls get pregnant outside of marriage. Fifty percent of high-school juniors and seniors are going to be falling down drunk and driving at least twice every month over the course of the school year. That's why alcohol-related accidents kill more students than any other cause of death. Further, a full ten percent of today's junior and senior high-schoolers are at high risk today in terms of committing suicide. You say, "Wait a minute, I don't have middle-schoolers or high-schoolers. I don't have to worry about that stuff."

If you wait until your kids get to that age to get concerned you've missed your greatest opportunity to help your children through this difficult time. Regardless of the age of your children, please, become aware of what you can do to protect your kids from these dangers.

In addition to these discouraging factors related to our children, marriages in our society are failing at an alarming rate. More than fifty percent of all marriages are ending in divorce. Many of those couples who remain married, are experiencing emotional isolation.

Many of us feel "pushed in" to a lot of things–we feel trapped. Within the context of the family, we often feel trapped in an unfulfilled marriage. Or we may be fighting to keep our heads above water as single parents. Maybe our kids are out of control and we don't know what to do or where to turn. Could it be that we started headlong into this family thing without really thinking where we ultimately wanted to end up?

I meet a large number of parents who have climbed what they thought was the ladder of success at great cost to their families only to find that it was leaning against the wrong wall. I suggest that the place to begin this discussion is at the beginning. What is success? When it's all said and done, what is really important in life?

> ### Successful families know their purpose as a family!

The best definition of individual success I know was developed by John Maxwell. He puts it this way in his best selling book *The Success Journey.* **"Success is knowing your purpose in life, growing to your maximum potential, and sowing seeds that benefit others."** This definition was of course written for the individual. However, successful families are made up of successful individuals–so success first and foremost is an inside job. We will deal with this aspect in the next section. For now, let me apply this definition to the family: Successful families know their purpose as a family, grow to their maximum potential, and beginning at home, sow seeds that benefit others.

At the Olympics, glory doesn't only belong to those who win. One author, Bud Greenspan

> ### The first and best victory is to conquer self. —Plato

writes in *100 Greatest Moments in Olympic History* several stories of determination, victory, and the power of inner desire and drive.

Dorando Pietri was in a state of collapse as he entered the stadium for the final yards of the 1908 marathon. The Italian fell five times before an official helped him cross the finish line. Pietri was disqualified, but his indomitable spirit made him an international celebrity. A similar display of courage enabled Derek Redmond of Great Britain to finish the 400 meters in 1992. Hobbled by a torn hamstring near the halfway point, Redmond hopped the rest of the way with the help of his father, Jim, who rushed from the stands to aid his son. And who could forget the sight of Tanzania's John Stephen Akhwari, his right leg bloody and bandaged, staggering into the stadium more than an hour behind the winner of the 1968 marathon? 'My country did not send me to Mexico City to start the race,' he said. 'They sent me to finish the race.'

What separated these Olympians from the rest? Why are we reading about them?

I suggest these athletes reflected three characteristics critical to the success of every family.

First, these Olympians were successful because they had a dream. When building a home, one of the first steps is deciding what you want your dream home to look like. Most couples find a picture in a magazine or see another house they really like. Before anything else is done they get a clear picture of the desired results.

These men all had a dream–they had goals. They wanted to be Olympic champions. It is also very evident from this account that these men had tried and had failed on other occasions. These men knew how to deal with setbacks and failure; these lessons can only be learned through the tough times. Now, that is very, very important because some of you, right now in terms of family, feel like a failure. Maybe you're divorced. unhappily married, or struggling with your children.

Please read carefully here; success is not synonymous with perfection and it does not mean that you don't mess up. It doesn't mean that you don't go through struggles or don't have down times. This is a very important concept that applies in every aspect of life.

The Olympians above were successful because they had a dream that moved them through the pain of competition. They wanted not only to compete, but to finish the race. Steven Covey, in his bestselling book *Seven Habits of Highly Effective People*, expresses this key principle this way, "Begin with the end in mind." If you want to be successful, you have to begin any family, business, or any other endeavor you set out to accomplish–with the end in mind. You have to get a clear picture of the destination in your mind before you begin the trip.

When I was in college I allowed my girlfriend to talk me into the incredibly stupid idea of running a marathon. Just in case you may not know, let me tell you what that is. A marathon is a twenty-six mile, 400 yard race. I did not say 2,600 yards, 26,000 yards, it is twenty-six stinking miles and 400 yards. Our objective wasn't to win. Our objective was to finish. We wanted to finish the race and be able to brag to our kids and our grandkids by saying, "I ran a marathon." I found out later what a total symbol of ignorance that was! We ran the marathon! I also want you to know I haven't jogged since the marathon. I now operate by what I call the heartbeat philosophy. Have you heard of it? You're going to love this–the heartbeat philosophy means that God has predetermined that everybody lives a certain number of heartbeats and when you use up that number of beats, you're dead. In my opinion, when you jog, you're unnecessarily wasting heartbeats. Just kidding of course! In order to run the marathon, we ran six miles, six days a week, and then for about a month before the marathon, we ran twenty

> *What are your dreams? For you? For your family?*

miles twice a week. The week prior to that marathon, I was in the best shape of my life. Toward the end of training, while I was on one of these twenty mile runs, I thought to myself at about seven or eight miles, "Not only am I going to finish this marathon, I'm breaking three hours." And at about ten miles I thought to myself, "Not only am I going to break three hours, I'm going to break two and a half." Then at about ten or twelve miles, I thought, "Not only am I going to break two and a half hours but I am going to win the marathon and I'll go on to win the Boston marathon, the New York marathon, and the gold medal in the Olympics." Then I started thinking, "Jerry, this is crazy–you're dreaming about jogging! How long has it been since you dreamed about what is really important?"

I realized I was dreaming about every area in my life except the ones that were truly important and valuable. I want to ask you an honest ques-

> *Do you dream, plan, and engage in those things that are "urgent" or those things that are "important?"*

tion. It's not my intention to make you feel guilty, but if it were somehow possible for me to sit down with you right now, individually, and look at that place where you record the key issues of your life, would we find two to five meaningful, specific goals that in the next thirty days or in the next six weeks you are going to accomplish? Have you established

> *Great potential and energy without a dream and focus is like an octopus on roller skates—plenty of movement— you just don't go anywhere.*

specific goals for your life? For your relationship with your spouse? For your children? As a family? Are there specific dreams and goals that you are trying to accomplish? If those specific dreams and goals aren't there,

then right now you're aiming at nothing and if you aim at nothing, you're going to hit it.

The reason we read the stories of these men in *Great Moments of Olympic History* is that their stories remind us of the importance of having a dream; in the midst of great challenge, their specific dreams and goals sustained them.

Successful families don't just happen.

Successful families happen because, through purposeful behavior, we begin with the end in mind. So, what are your dreams for your relationship with your spouse?

- ◆ A dream for intimacy?
- ◆ A dream for better communication?
- ◆ A dream that the relationship will be marked by integrity?
- ◆ A dream that we will pass on our values to the next generation?

What are your goals for your children and your grandchildren? I want my children to be respectful, honest, self-disciplined, with high moral standards. I met two parents once who wanted to pass on to their son a commitment to moral purity. It was their desire that he wait to have sex until after marriage. Watching their son maintain the commitment was a joy.

One day as a senior in high school, he was playing in a tennis tournament. When it came time for lunch, he realized that he had left his food on the bus. As he boarded the bus to retrieve his meal, he was met by a gorgeous blond cheerleader and teammate. She pulled him down into her lap and, in the words of *On Golden Pond*, initiated some serious "sucking face." He quickly realized that if he stayed on the bus, he was going to get off without something that was very valuable to him. He stopped mid-kiss and stood up; as he stood, she started unbuttoning his tennis shorts. He grabbed her arm and said, "I'm saving this for the person I'm going to spend my life with." He then quickly got off the bus. Six years later, his wedding night was unbelievably special for him and his wife. But, do you know why it was special? It was special because his mom and his dad had a dream for moral purity and they made a commitment to help him achieve it.

> *Every great achievement is the story of a flaming heart.*
> *—Harry S Truman*

So what are your dreams for your kids? Think about it–moral purity, integrity, honesty, genuine love, becoming other-oriented? A commitment to self-discipline?

Here's the point: Successful families, successful people, dream. They begin with the end in mind. They get a clear picture of what they want their house to look like before they finalize the blueprints or start the structure.

> *Successful families dream.*

The second step to building a successful family is to develop a plan. When building a home, after you get a clear picture of what you want, the next step is finding the right architect to design your dream home. He develops it in every detail in what we call a blueprint before the ground is ever touched. Your dreams, along with the plan to accomplish them, is the blueprint for your family.

It's important not just that we know where we're going, but that we know how we're going to get there. I have close friends who, like the men previously mentioned, were Olympic athletes. Their plan for preparation was nothing short of incredible. It impacted every area of their life–diet, relocating to a training village, and a demanding physical training regimen.

> *Everyone who takes a shower has an idea; it's what you do with it when you get out that makes the difference.*

Planning for a successful family takes the same kind of thoughtful planning. For example, how do you build bridges of communication in the home? How do you establish identity and build self-worth and self-esteem? What is it that is so different about children and teenagers today? After all, you must understand them to be able to try and make a difference as a parent or a grandparent. Then what about discipline? Have you ever been frustrated about that issue? How do you meaningfully provide discipline and boundaries without creating a negative atmosphere in your home? How do we avoid this common scenario: "Johnny, I want you to go upstairs, do your list and get ready to go to bed." You come back ten minutes later, "Johnny, I told you I want you to go upstairs, do your list, get ready and go to bed. You haven't even moved." Then, fifteen minutes later, "Johnny, I want you to get upstairs right now."

When I was growing up, it would have been at about this time that my mom would have taught me about time travel: "Son, if you do not do that right now, I'm going to knock you into next week!" Back to Johnny, he doesn't move until you finally turn three shades of purple and yell. Have you ever had that type of experience? As a parent, how can you develop

> *Before everything else, getting ready is the secret of success.*
> *—Henry Ford*

a plan for discipline that not only removes this kind of frustration, but results in self-discipline for the child?

This book is about developing a plan for all of the above and much more. You will learn how to develop and to maintain intimacy in marriage, how to grow personally, and how to listen effectively.

But there is a third thing about the three Olympians from our previous story–not only did they have a dream and not only did they have a plan, these guys were willing to pay the price to achieve their dream. In fact, it was that trait that made them heroes.

The third step in building a successful family is to make the sacrifice. It costs to have a successful family. You know what we don't understand in America? The price tag for success in the family includes serious sacrifice. We want the best for our marriage. We want the best for our family, for our kids. We want our kids to be respectful, honest, have integrity, and learn enduring values. We live in an instant microwave society, but healthy families demand a slow-cooking crock pot.

My daughter wants to become a high-school cheerleader. In today's world, that is a whole lot more about gymnastics than it is about the ability to cheer. Paige and I were on our way home from cheer factory on a night when she was pretty discouraged over her progress. She said, "You know Dad, I'm so frustrated with this," and I responded, "It makes me absolutely no difference whether you ever become a cheerleader or not. Now if that is your dream and it's important to you, then I am happy to help you–I'll wave the flag and cheer you on. Paige, what is important to me is that you learn to dream a dream, decide what you have to do to get there, and then be willing to pay the price."

> *Courage is being scared to death and saddling up anyway.*
> *—John Wayne*

Imagine a man crossing the desert. He starts with more than enough water and food, but it takes longer to get across the desert than he expects. Three days after he runs out of food and water, he crosses a sand dune and he's desperate, just on the edge of death. He sees this rickety well shack and he knows it's not a mirage because a mirage would look better than this. So he walks up to the well shack, goes inside and begins to pump the old rusty well–nothing happens. Just at that moment, out of the corner of his eye, he sees a rusty bucket and this inscription: "Empty the contents of the bucket into the well to prime the pump and be sure to fill it up for the next traveler."

Now he has a serious dilemma. There is enough water, although it's dirty and murky, to survive. But what if the well doesn't work? He knows that he wouldn't make it without water. But, what if the well does work? What if he primes the pump and the well works? Then, he gets to take a bath, he gets clean water, he gets to have all the water he wants. More importantly, he can fill it up so that the next person lives to have the same choice as he had.

I love what Zig Zigler says, "You'll never find fulfillment in committing a selfish act."

You want to be happy? You want to find success? Help the people around you, the people you love, get what they want out of life and you'll get what you want out of life. In America, it's a drop-dead proven fact that the more money you make, the more famous you become, the more influential you are, or the more educated you are: The greater the chance you will put a pistol in your mouth, pull the trigger, and blow your brains out, because none of those things will make you happy.

You might become a scratch golfer, but it won't make you happy. You could spend all your spare time shopping, fishing, skiing, hiking, or whatever it is you want to do. You can spend money that you don't have to buy things that you don't need, to please people that you don't like–and it's still not going to make you happy.

But if you will help your wife or husband, if you will help your kids become the best they can be, you will be sowing seeds that benefit others, and you will see them grow to their maximum potential. Then, I promise you, you'll get what you want out of life and a lot more.

What are your dreams for yourself? What are your dreams for your spouse and your marriage? What are your dreams for your children and your family?

What are your plans to accomplish your dreams?

What is your purpose? Are you growing toward your maximum potential? Are you sowing seeds that benefit others?

> *Success is knowing your purpose in life, growing to your maximum potential, and sowing seeds that benefit others.*
> *—John C. Maxwell*

Put on Your Construction Hat and Let's Go to Work!

Consulting the Blueprint
What concepts from this chapter can I work on, learn, or practice?

These concepts will increase the value of my family in what ways?

What can I do to apply these principles in a practical way?

Building Blocks for My Home
With concepts from this chapter, what are practical steps I can take to build my family and create a "healthier" home?
One:

Two:

Three:

Basic Blocks For Building

1.) What are your dreams for yourself? Think about creating a balanced life as you dream–creating a balance between the social, emotional, physical, and spiritual aspects. What are your personal goals? Professional goals?

2.) What are some of the dreams your spouse has? What are some of the dreams that your spouse has for the marriage? What are your dreams for your spouse? What are your dreams for the marriage?

3.) What are your dreams for your children? What are your five-year goals for them? What are your dreams for your family? Your five-year goals for your family? Ten-year goals?

4.) What are your plans to accomplish these dreams?

5.) What is your purpose individually, as a couple, as a family? Are you growing toward your maximum potential? Are you sowing seeds that benefit others?

6.) How can we improve and grow together as a family?

Section Two

Building Your Successful Home

Goethe once said,
"He is happiest, king or peasant,
who finds happiness at home"
and Goethe knew–because he
never found it.
—Elbert Hubbard

Chapter II.
Laying Your Foundation–Success is an Inside Job

The most important part of any home is the foundation. During the mid-eighties my wife, Debra, and I moved to Jackson, Mississippi. While house shopping, we discovered the impact of red clay on the foundation of a home. Many builders, in an attempt to maximize profit, would cut corners on soil preparation prior to pouring the foundation. We looked at house after house that appeared incredible on the outside only to find cracks in interior walls or doors that no longer functioned properly due to a shifting foundation. When you are building a successful family, it is exactly the same. Without a solid foundation, everything we strive to accomplish in family life is in jeopardy of falling down around us. Our families may look great on the outside, but it is only a matter of time before the interior cracks begin to appear.

The first step in laying a solid foundation is for each individual in the family to grow to their maximum potential. **Success is, first and foremost, success with self.** It is an inside job! While we can influence the other members of our family, we have absolute control over ourselves. This chapter will not be exhaustive by any stretch of the imagination;

there are entire books and book series on this subject alone. However, here are a few suggestions for a life of personal growth.

> *Success is an inside job!*

There are five dimensions of our lives that must be continually developed to achieve maximum success.

The Volitional Dimension—The power to choose.

Healthy families are made up of healthy individuals who exercise their power to choose. Many of the theories of the world tell us that we do not have the "power to choose." Many of the psychological disciplines say we are "pre-determined." The basic theories are these:

Genetic Determinism—This basically means that our ancestors determine our behavior through the genetic code passed from one generation to the next. Many people today accept this theory as fact. For example, a lady I worked with once told me: "My mother had a short fuse, and her mother had a bad temper; that's just the way I am." With this statement, she relieved herself of the responsibility of venting on the people she loves the most. "I just can't help it; this just runs in the family." No one would disagree that genetics powerfully influence us. Many of the wonderful physical traits and talents we possess come genetically from our ancestors. However, they do not determine us. In the illustration above regarding uncontrollable anger, the woman who said this was able to control her anger and responses at work or she would not have still had a job. She was influenced, but not determined, by genetics.

Psychic Determinism—This is the Freudian idea that the "child is father to the man." This theory presupposes that the way we are raised by our parents during the first five or six years of our lives determines our behavior as adults. Again, there is no question that these early years influence us greatly, but they do not determine us. We can choose our response to those influences.

Social Determinism—If you have ever studied psychology, you will recognize the letters SR or stimulus response. Behaviorists repeatedly ring a bell while feeding a dog. Eventually, every time the dog hears a bell, its saliva glands begin to work due to the association of a ringing bell and being fed. They call this stimulus response and suggest that just like animals we are socially determined through this process. Again, I disagree! The power to choose means that as humans, we have the power to separate the stimulus from our response. There is no question that stimulus response influences us and, at times, powerfully. But it does not determine us.

Again, there is no question that all these powerfully influence us, but for us to grow to our maximum potential we must first accept responsibility to choose our behavior. The power to choose is what separates people from animals. We have the ability to reason. While animals only react to their environment, humans have the ability to respond to any person or situation based on their values. As people, we can determine our purpose in life, choose

> ### We are only as good as our private standards.

our values, grow to our maximum potential and add value to others along the way. Healthy families are made up of healthy individuals who exercise and develop their ability to choose.

The Physical Dimension—Choosing to take care of our bodies.

This requires physical exercise three or four times a week for thirty minutes each time. While the physical benefits are good, the greatest benefits are emotional, which results in the reduction of stress and an enhanced self-esteem. A good physical workout should include:

- ◆ Endurance—aerobic exercises, getting your heart rate up and keeping it up for twenty minutes, three to four times per week through biking, swimming, walking, or jogging.
- ◆ Flexibility—stretching before and after aerobic exercise.
- ◆ Strength—toning through calisthenics or weights.

> * Before beginning an exercise regimen, see your doctor for a physical to make sure there are no health issues that would make the above suggestions dangerous for you. For example, you would not want to begin an aerobic workout if you had blockage in the arteries of your heart.

> **Stress is when you wake up screaming and you realize you weren't asleep.**

The Mental/Emotional Dimension—This means developing both sides of our brains.

The left side of our brain is the logical/reasoning side. The right side is the feeling/sensing or more emotional side. Most people stop learning after getting out of school. There are several reasons for this and one of the most prevalent is the television. In most homes, the television is on forty to forty-five hours each week. While the television could, if used properly, serve our values, for the most part it is a plug-in drug. It imperceptibly shapes our values and is addictive. If you don't think so, just try to do without it for thirty days. I am not suggesting that we get rid of it. Rather, that we ask ourselves: How can we use this powerful medium of television to serve our families and help them accomplish their purpose while growing to their maximum potential? Just think, except for the books we read, conferences we attend, and the experiences we are exposed to, we will be the same in thirty years as we are today.

> **Thinking is hard work . . . that's why so few do it.**
> **—Albert Einstein**

The following are suggestions to develop the mental/emotional dimension:

♦ Read great books. One who chooses not to read is no better off than one who can't read at all. This person chooses a self-imposed illiteracy. If you have not been reading, begin with a goal for a book a month. An occasional novel is fine, but read great biographies and self-help books as well. I suggest you read at least two books per year on marriage and family.

♦ Listen to tapes. If you spend a lot of time in your car, this is a wise use of your time.

♦ Attend good conferences.

- Plug into continuing education.
- Write great letters and keep a journal.
- Use the internet to serve your values.
- Engage in problem solving and planning.
- Get into the arts and nature.
- Laugh every day. Look for the humor in life.

> *Laughing is good exercise; it's like jogging on the inside.*

The Spiritual Dimension—This is where the leadership of our lives is developed.

It is here that we develop our character, core values, and make our decisions concerning the nature and purpose of life–our worldview. In the last section of this book, there will be a more full discussion to help you think through this area in more depth. Here are a few suggestions to consider:

- Develop a personal mission statement–decide what you want to accomplish in life.
- Develop goals from your mission statement and strategies to reach them.

The Social Dimension—This is where we take a close look at our environment.

People we spend a lot of time with have a huge impact on our lives. If you will give me fifteen minutes with a person's closest friends, I will be able to tell much about where their heart really is. Those with whom we spend the bulk of our time have more to do with the way we think, feel, act and react than almost any other factor. It's great for all of us to ask often: Does my environment serve my purpose and values? Do the people I spend time with, and the places I go help or hinder me in being what I dream to be?

All success begins with yourself. It is without a doubt the foundation for a successful life and family. I find that all of my family and professional victories have had their roots in the area of personal growth. Without exception, every failure in my life has had its roots right here as well. Every failure can be traced back to a time when I neglected to develop one of these five areas. Therefore, I fight daily to protect the time it takes to develop these five dimensions of my life.

> ### *Growing old is mandatory; growing up is optional.*

I challenge you to commit one hour a day to begin working on these five dimensions. Just one hour in twenty-four that will add value to every waking moment of your life.

This investment in the foundation of your home will be the best investment of your life.

Put on Your Construction Hat and Let's Go to Work!

Consulting the Blueprint

What concepts from this chapter can I work on, learn, or practice?

These concepts will increase the value of my family in what ways?

What can I do to apply these principles in a practical way?

Additional Suggested Resources:

Covey, Stephen. *The Seven Habits of Highly Effective People.*
Franklin Covey Planner.
MacDonald, Gordon. *Ordering Your Private World.*
Maxwell, John C. *The Success Journey.*
Maxwell, John C. *The 21 Indispensable Qualities of a Leader.*

Chapter III.
Building the Walls—A Healthy Marriage

After laying a solid foundation, the next step in building a home is putting up the walls. Walls protect the home from the outside elements and provide structure inside. Healthy marriages are like the walls of a home in that they provide protection from the unwanted outside influences that can destroy families. Additionally, they are the primary source of security or structure within the family. A healthy marriage is marked by intimacy, but too often, the experience is one of isolation.

More than fifty percent of marriages today end in divorce.

Twenty-five percent of the people who stay married experience incredible unfulfillment, frustration, and emotional isolation.

How does a relationship so quickly move from the excitement of the wedding day to isolation of the partners or disintegration of the marriage?

Five stages of the disintegration of a relationship

There are five stages of the disintegration of a relationship; learn the stages and watch for the signs. Signs are important. They warn us of impending danger. One of my favorite signs was posted on a barbed-wire fence. It read: "Warning, absolutely no trespassing. Trespassers will be prosecuted to the fullest extent of the law." Strangely it was signed, "Sisters of Mercy." In important relationships, learn these stages and watch for the signs.

First, there is the romantic stage. At this stage, a couple is so in love. At this point, love is a feeling you feel when you feel a feeling you have never felt before. All the problems of the marriage will be solved by these overwhelming feelings of love. Things that may eventually drive one partner or the other stark-raving mad about their mate are not even noticed at this stage. Truly, love is blind.

Second, there is the rigorous stage. That's when the couple begins to really work at the marriage. There are twinges of disappointment over those things that will eventually become a major source of irritation.

But, these twinges of disappointment are extinguished quickly by the overwhelming feelings of love.

Third, there is the reality stage. This is where reality really begins to set in. Things that once used to be minor irritations become major sources of frustration and anger. It's at this point that most couples discover the double-edged dagger–love is blind.

"Love is blind" obviously means that in the beginning, we don't notice things that will eventually drive us crazy. However, if you don't work to cultivate the sources of security in your marriage, a point will come when the only things you'll notice about your spouse are those things you don't like.

Fourth, there is the retaliation stage. The anger and the disappointment leads to a time where we lash out emotionally, and even sometimes, physically.

Finally, there is the rejection stage. This is where one or both spouses believe the only way to solve the problems of the relationship is to end it. Here is the strange thing: Many, many times when we try to solve the problems through divorce, we end up creating far greater problems socially, financially, and in many other ways for everyone involved!

There are three basic principles you must follow in order to build and maintain intimacy in marriage.

First, you must seek to understand and value differences. Men and women are different in incalculable ways. In the early seventies, during the height of the ERA movement, that statement would have made people angry. But now, people agree; men and women are just wired differently.

For example, men and women are different in the way they approach going to the restroom. For men, this is a private activity. For ladies, it necessitates support groups. I used to enjoy the privacy of that experience until I got married. Now my wife just barges in; it's at that moment she always wants to solve family problems. Ladies generally make the announcement, "I need to go; does anybody else need to go?" Men and women are just different.

The primary way that men and women are different is that men are logical and women are emotional.

I am not an emotional person; my wife is. She gets excited, bounces off the walls, and everybody knows she's excited. Last year there was a time when I did not talk to my wife for six months. We weren't mad and we weren't angry; I just didn't want to interrupt her. Men and women– we're just different. My wife likes to go to the butterfly exhibit at the museum. She likes to watch *Touched by an Angel*. I like to see cars go over the cliff and blow up. My wife thinks that newborn babies are pretty. I think they look like aliens. I was there when my two children were born and I said to the doctor, "They're not done–put them back in."

> *Dates are for having fun, and people should use them to get to know each other. Even boys have something to say if you listen long enough. —Lynette, age 8*

Men and women are different in the way they approach self-worth and self-esteem. I get on airplanes all over the world. I've never heard a man begin a conversation with, "You're not going to believe what's going on with my wife and my kids. . ." They never do that. They always start with a question like: "What do you do?" Then, they begin to talk about what they do. They say something like, "When I bought this company they were doing $30,000 and now we're doing $300,000." Men get their self-worth and self-esteem through building this and fixing that.

Ladies, on the other hand, get their self-worth and self-esteem largely through their relationships with their husbands and their children. John Gray, the author of *Men Are From Mars, Women Are From Venus*, entitled a chapter on this subject, "Mr. Fix-it and the Home Improvement Committee." Imagine that the husband is coming home from work and the wife is fixing the meal. Maybe she was

> *Most men are brainless, so you might have to try more than one to find a live one. —Angie, age 10*

working too, but for now she is preparing supper and begins talking about a problem at the office or maybe a problem with one of the kids. What does the man do? We traditionally listen for about three or four minutes, and after we think that we have the picture, we begin to suggest a solution. "Have you thought about this? Have you thought about that?"

Listen men, here's a tip: She didn't bring the situation up because she wanted you to fix it. She's not interested in the solution; that's why none of them work. What she's interested in is getting your nose out of the paper and away from the television and getting you to focus on her. She needs and wants a conversation. She's interested in the relationship.

Men and women are just wired completely differently. Men need admiration and women need to be wives and moms. Men get into the car on the way to go somewhere and it's obvious that we don't have a clue where we're going. So, the wife always asks, "Honey did you look at the map before we left?" Or she makes the suggestion, "Why don't you stop and ask for directions?" You see, she's a mom; she needs to be "a mom." Please ladies, there are two things men don't do: We don't look at maps and we don't stop and ask for directions. And ladies, I will give you a new perspective. You need to get excited that we don't do those two things. Think about it this way–there are places in this world you would never see if men looked at maps and asked for directions.

If you spend your marriage trying to change the other person, trying to do your number on your spouse, you will end up in isolation. You need to seek to understand and value the differences. The more you can understand and value the differences, the more you can experience intimacy. Intimacy simply means "into me see." The desire of a couple is to experience intimacy–opening

> ***You cannot change somebody else—you can only change yourself. And sometimes, <u>that</u> makes all the difference!***

up and seeing inside of each other. The flip-side of intimacy is isolation.

Isolation is frustrating and results in a lack of real fulfillment in the marriage relationship. We could spend hundreds of pages on this issue alone. If you really want to understand and value the differences, pick up a couple of books and seek to understand the differences. Please understand, very few marriage partners have affairs on purpose. Also, 99.9 percent of all affairs have nothing to do with sex. They have to do with unmet emotional and physical needs. Men and women are different, and we have to understand and value the differences if we're going to experience a fulfilling marriage.

Another thing we must do in order to experience intimacy is remove the obstacles to communication. Our problem in communicating is not in talking. All of us can talk well. Our problem in communicating is listening. We're not listening to each other or even trying to communicate that we're listening

> *Be slow to speak, quick to hear, and slow to anger.*

to each other. There are five levels of listening. Most often, the majority of us are practicing the first level of listening–which is not listening at all: The first level is simply ignoring.

It's quite probable that we don't do this on purpose; we don't ignore because we're mean or angry. We just emotionally are somewhere else; we're at the office or we're still with a friend or we're thinking about something else; therefore our family is not getting our attention. But it is painful nonetheless. It can be very damaging. Second, there is pretend listening. We try to communicate that we're listening, but we're not. Third, there is selective listening–this is what we do with those who talk a lot. Moms have to do this to some degree with preschoolers.

Then comes attentive listening. This is where we are attending and genuinely listening for content.

The fifth and most powerful level of listening is empathetic listening. That is where you are empathizing–really experiencing the words and feeling the emotions of the person speaking. You express this with your eyes, look for emotion, and try to reflect back what you see; anger, frustration, hurtfulness, disappointment, etc. People generally feel listened to and valued when this type of listening takes place.

One of the biggest problems in communication is that most of us don't take the time to really listen when people are talking. Rather, we're thinking about what we're going to say next in response. For example, anytime you catch yourself saying, "Oh yeah, I can relate to that. Let me tell you about this experience I had one time." Communication has not occurred. Instead of focusing on what someone else is saying and giving them undivided attention, we're thinking about what we are going to say next. Miscommunication is often unbelievably painful. A guy moved his business to a brand new location. A friend thoughtfully sent flowers and a note. He opened the card and it read, "Rest in peace." Now obviously somebody made a mistake because he knew his friend would not have sent him a note that said, "Rest in peace." He got on the phone and called the florist and angrily said, "What's the problem? I got flowers that said 'Rest in peace' and I know that's not the message my friend sent to my grand opening." The florist said, "I know you might be frustrated and we're really sorry. But take courage and be assured that you're better off than someone at a funeral later today who will open a note that says 'Congratulations on your new location.'"

Anytime we don't genuinely listen, miscommunication occurs, and in the family, miscommunication is a lot more serious than an inappropriate card. In fact, when miscommunication occurs in the family, people with whom we want to connect are so incredibly frustrated because they're pouring their heart out to us as a spouse or a child, and we miss the obvious.

The Lone Ranger and Tonto put up their tent and got settled in for a good night's rest. A few hours later, the Lone Ranger looks up in the middle of the night and sees millions of stars. He wakes up Tonto and says, "Tonto, what do you see?" Tonto responds, "I see millions and millions and billions of stars." The Lone Ranger says, "What does that mean to you, Tonto?" And Tonto says, "Kemo sabe that means to me, astronomically, that we live in a vast universe with billions of stars and galaxies, etc. Theologically, that means to me that we have an unbelievable God who created all of this. Meteorologically, that means to me that tomorrow, it is probably going to be sunny and very hot. What does it mean to you kemo sabe?"

The Lone Ranger responded, "Tonto, you idiot! It means that someone has stolen our tent!"

Sometimes in the midst of the communication process, our children sit down and they pour their heart out, or our wife is pouring her heart out. We respond by saying, "Oh yeah, I can relate to that," then we start reading our paper and they know we didn't even listen.

My wife and I made two commitments a long, long time ago that have forever changed our marriage. We made a commitment that we would never say anything to each other that we did not absolutely 100 percent mean. My father had an explosive personality. He would allow his anger to build up and when he blew up, he would say horribly cutting and sarcastic things to my mom and us kids. I learned later that he didn't mean those things and that fifteen minutes later he

> ### *If you are going to have intimacy, you must <u>connect</u> with important people in your life.*

wouldn't even remember that he had said them. However, the damage was done. We can never "take back" words once they are spoken.

Why is it that we feel the freedom to blow up with our spouse or with our kids and say horribly, cutting things? We don't mean them but we say them. We would never do that at our job.

"Wait a minute," you might say, "I just have a bad temper; I can't control myself." You probably still have a job and if most of us acted at our jobs like we do in our families, we wouldn't be employed. My wife and I made a commitment that if we don't mean it, we don't say it. That means there are times when we get frustrated and we have to finish the conversation later when we can do it calmly: We choose to honor our commitment to say only what we mean.

The second commitment we made to each other is that we will never let the sun go down on an unresolved conflict. At the end of the day, we solve the problem or resolve the conflict to meet the expectations of both of us. I have to confess to you there was a time last year when we didn't sleep for about eight months, but we made a commitment and we've kept it!

I will never forget being in Boston. We got to this intersection and my host said to me, "Jerry, you're not going to believe this. At this intersection several years ago in a dense fog, a tractor trailer and a truck collided and then, because of the fog, there was vehicle collision upon another, upon another, and over the course of about forty-five to fifty minutes, more than 100 cars were piled up. It was at that time the worst traffic pile up in American history. It took several days before traffic could pass through this intersection." The thought occurred to me as I heard this story; that's exactly where so many of our families are today.

Some of you are at that same spot right now. Your husband, your wife, or one of your children did something to hurt you, and you have not forgiven them. Maybe you made a promise and have not kept it, and because of your ego, you have not been able to deal with it or ask for forgiveness. Often, one insensitivity upon another occurs until the communication in a family is ruptured.

We must allow selfish behavior to go by the wayside. There is no room in a healthy family or healthy home for selfish people. Some of you are thinking, "If you had any idea what my husband has done to hurt me, my husband had an affair." "If you had any idea what my child has done, my teenager has ripped my heart out." "If you had any idea what people have done to me, you would not be asking me to forgive them and let it go." It's not what people do to us that does the damage; it's our response to what they do to us that does the damage.

> **There is no room in a healthy family, or in a healthy home for selfish people.**

Imagine a man in West Texas who heard a rattlesnake in the bush. This guy was a complete idiot. Now, I don't like snakes–in my opinion, the only good snake is a dead snake. The only way a snake is going to get dead if I have anything to do with it, is if I have a double-barreled twelve-gauge shotgun and I can help him get dead from a distance. This guy had a machete in his hand and with the machete he was going to cut the head off the snake. The man wasn't very good with the machete. Instead of cutting the head off the snake, he cut the snake in half and the half with the head bit him.

Now I want to ask you a question–would this man die from the snake bite? The answer to that question is no. It's not fun to get bit by a rattlesnake, but if you put ice on the bite, take anti-venom and elevate the wound, you're not going to die. But if he said, "The snake bit me; the snake is going to get what is coming to it," and chased the rattlesnake through the bush, the man would be dead! What would have killed him? The snake bite? No. His response to the rattlesnake and its bite would be what killed him.

> **Forgiveness is essential!**

It's not what people do to us that does the damage. It's our response to what people do to us that does the damage. What we need to do when someone hurts us is suck out the poison and deal with the hurt in a way that restores health into a meaningful relationship.

Intimacy = Into Me See

If you want to have intimacy in your marriage–if you want to have a healthy family–you're going to have to be willing to forgive. Because I promise you in every single family, there will be mistakes. Every single individual involved in the family is going to mess up. If you ever find the perfect family, don't join it; you'll mess it up. Remove obstacles to communication.

Finally, intimacy takes commitment. If you're going to have intimacy you will have to work at your relationship like you work at everything else that is important to you. That goes contrary to our world's definition of what love is. In our society, "Love is a feeling you feel when you feel the feeling you never felt before." Have you ever heard people say that they have "fallen in love?" People in our society talk about falling in love all the time. Or they say on the other end of happiness, "I'm getting a divorce because I have fallen out of love with my wife." You don't fall in love; you fall into a hole. You fall into a lake. You don't fall out of love; you fall out of a tree. In genuine love, you grow together as you work at your relationship, and you grow apart through neglect. To make marriage work, you must work at the marriage like you work at everything else that is important to you.

It has been well said, In marriage, you can either be happy or right." You're not going to be both; you can either be happy or right. Some of the hardest work I do in marriage is remembering this profound truth. How true!

My wife and I were talking in bed the other night and she said, "Jerry, I am so cold. What did you do? Turn the thermostat down to sixty? I mean, what is the deal? Just trying to save money? I am freezing." Now I hadn't touched the thermostat but she griped and griped and finally (remember you can either be happy or right), I went over to the thermostat and looked–I didn't touch it at all! I just got close, then got back in bed. After about ten minutes, my wife said, "Thank you so much; it's so much better."

Now, I wanted to say–I didn't touch it. Remember, you can either be happy or right. Another ten minutes, and she said, "Jerry what did you do?" and she's kicking off the covers, "Did you turn it up to ninty?" Remember, I haven't touched it. I went back over, I just got close to touching it, then, I got back in bed again. "Oh, thank you so much." We slept peacefully the rest of the night.

> ## In marriage, you can either be happy or right.

You can be happy or right.

A gentleman walked up to me and said, "I'm miserable; my marriage is over. What I'm planning to do is divorce my wife and marry my administrative assistant. Will you help me with the details?"

"Really?" I asked, "How did you come to this conclusion?" He said, "Listen Jerry, you wouldn't believe my wife–she's driving me crazy. I'm divorcing my wife and marrying my assistant; I'm so in love with her."

You never find happiness through committing a selfish act. If you invest in your spouse and children helping them find what they want and need in life...if you help other people to fulfill their dreams, then you'll always find what you're looking for in life.

This gentleman was on the double-edged dagger of "love is blind." You see, he didn't remember any of the things that led him to grow into love with his wife and marry her in the first place. He had forgotten the things he loved about his wife. He had forgotten because he failed to cultivate the sources of security in his marriage; therefore, he only saw the

> ## You never find happiness through committing a selfish act.

things he hated in his wife. At the same time, he was on the front edge of the double-edged dagger with his administrative assistant. The only things he could see about her were the things he loved. He couldn't see the things that would eventually drive him stark-raving mad later. I said to him, "Listen, if you make this brain-dead choice," (I got my counseling skills from reading *How to Win Friends and Influence People*.), "you'll be calling me in five or six years and having the same conversation I had with a friend just last week." He was leaving wife number four for wife number five. Just change the names and dates. All the conversations were the same. "If you leave your wife and the mother of your children for your administrative assistant, in five or six years you're going to see only the things in *her* you hate and someone else will come along who is everything she's not."

> *To be successful is to be helpful, caring, and constructive, to make everything and everyone you touch a little bit better. The best thing you have to give is yourself.*
> *—Norman Vincent Peale*

Let's be honest. This whole marriage and family thing can get very intense, can't it? It's hard work to have an awesome family. It takes a tremendous amount of energy and it's a never ending job. One noted author calls it the "straight life." It's changing diapers. It's mowing the yard. It's doing your taxes. It's being responsible with your money. It's working fifty weeks a year and taking a two-week vacation, and giving a lot to your family. It's taking care of the kids. It's simply doing the stuff that must be done.

The answer to the straight life is not an affair or a new marriage to someone else. Rather, the answer is to build fun, romance, and excitement into the marriage you have now. It's to remember what led you to grow into love and get married in the first place and to cultivate those sources as security. It's to work at this relationship like you work at everything else that's important to you.

> *No age is good to get married at . . . You got to be a fool to get married!*
> *—Freddie, age 6*

I have a friend who is a lot like me in that he hates to fish. Now if you're a fisherman, I don't want you to feel attacked. I'm an athlete. You give me a couple of hours off, and I want to play golf, tennis, basketball or football. If the game involves a ball, I like it. Given a couple of hours off, I want to go out and actively do something. When you go fishing, you are standing on the bank or sitting in a boat waiting for some psychotic fish to be active on your hook. Now if you get excited about fishing, I don't want you to feel offended. By the way, I have a definition for a fisherman: A fisherman is a jerk on one end of the line waiting for a jerk on the other. (Just kidding!)

My friend had a couple of co-workers who loved to fish and after two years of constant harassment, he agreed to go fishing with them in the mountains of Colorado on the Arkansas River. His two fanatical fishing friends stripped down to their swimming trunks and slipped into the ice water in inner tubes. My friend was infinitely smarter than they were; he sat down with a jar of lemonade, a ham and cheese sandwich, a bag of chips, and went to sleep. After a couple of hours, his co-workers came back and said, "Hey, did you catch any fish?" He held up his rod showing them he didn't have any.

"What about you guys? Did you catch any fish?" They held up a stringer of twenty-seven unbelievable rainbow trout. On the way back to

> **He didn't cast his rod— and he didn't catch any fish.**

the cabin, he asked them, "How many times did you cast your rod to catch those fish?" They replied, "Probably 2,500 to 3,000 times." My friend, on the other hand, didn't cast his rod at all and didn't catch any fish.

In the same regard, marriage and family are much like fishing. It makes no difference how much you want to have an awesome marriage. It makes no difference how much you want your kids to grow up and be the winners you dream for them to be. It makes no difference how much you want your family to be the best it can possibly be. Until you are willing to work at those things like you work at everything else you value in this life, those things are not ever going to happen.

If you want intimacy, understand and value the differences. Remove the obstacles for communication, and be willing to work at intimacy like you would work at anything else you value.

A little girl was going through the check out line at the grocery store when she saw a cheap string of pearls for $1.98. "Mom, will you please buy me those pearls?" The mom, trying to teach her responsibility, said,

"Honey, every week you get an allowance and every week you make money. If you want the pearls, you need to buy them yourself."

So, the next week, with her allowance and what she could make from doing chores for the neighbors, she bought the pearls and was so unbelievably proud. She wore them to church, school, out in the neighborhood, and everywhere else you can imagine except for the swimming pool and the bathtub because that made them turn green. They were cheap imitations but, she was proud. Every night, her dad would put her to bed, and kiss her goodnight. One night, he walked in and said, "Honey, do you really love me?" She said, "Daddy, I love you more than life itself." He said, "Then, honey, give me your pearls."

She said, "Daddy, I love you; I love you more than life itself, but I can't give you my pearls. Daddy, I'll give you my horse Dolly; you know that's my favorite horse."

He said, "No, if you won't give me your pearls, I'm not interested."

About a week later, he asked again, "Honey, do you love me? Do you really love me?" She said, "Daddy, you know I love you; I love you more than anything." He said, "Give me your pearls." She said, "Daddy, I can't give you my pearls but I'll give you my baby doll; it's my favorite toy. But I cannot give you my pearls."

"No thank you," he said.

The next night, he walked into her room. He saw his daughter sitting Indian-style in the middle of her bed with big tears rolling down her cheeks. He asked, "What's wrong honey?" and she said, "Daddy, I love you; I love you more than anything," and out of her little sweaty palm, she dropped her most prized possession–her pearls–into her Daddy's hand and said, "I just want you to know I love you Daddy."

As he took the pearls, in the same motion he brought out of his back pocket a gorgeous blue velvet case with a string of beautiful, real, cultured pearls. As he placed them around her neck, he said, "I love you too, sweetheart."

The first time he asked for those cheap trinkets, he had the real thing to put in its place. Many of us are holding tightly to cheap imitations when just on the other side of a sacrificial commitment to our spouse and family is the real thing. Life's $1.98 pearls will never result in the happiness, significance, and fulfillment we're looking for. Just as the walls of your home provide protection and structure, the marriage relationship provides protection and structure for your family. The next step is to put on the roof.

Put on Your Construction Hat and Let's Go to Work!

Consulting the Blueprint
What concepts from this chapter can I work on, learn, or practice?

These concepts will increase the value of my family in what ways?

What can I do to apply these principles in a practical way?

Building Blocks for My Home
With concepts from this chapter, what are practical steps I can take to build my family and create a "healthier" home?
One:

Two:

Three:

Basic Blocks For Building

I. Be a mate, not a counselor. Be a cheerleader, not a judge. Be a co-worker, not a boss. Be software, not a system error. Be a coach, not an umpire. Be freedom, not a ball and chain. Be fire, not water. Be hope, not a red flag. Be a friend to your spouse, not a parent. Be a helper, not a slave driver. Be a complement, not a competitor.

II. Love languages are a part of the makeup of every individual and marriage. Learn to communicate with each other in a balance from the love languages but start with each other's dominant language. Following is a sample of ways to communicate in the love languages for a husband to a wife followed by a wife to her husband.

III. Ways to Show Love to Your Wife (by love language)

    1.) Create and Continually Enhance Meaning and Value for Her:

-Never embarrass her.	-Always be accessible to her.
-Be faithful to her.	-Remember important dates.
-Make her a priority.	-Set aside time together (date).
-Support and encourage her.	-Put her picture up and brag on her.

    2.) Encourage Her with Your Words:

-Send her card/love notes.	-Sing a message to voice mail.
-Write her a poem.	-Compliment her cooking.
-Tell her you're lucky.	-Be thankful and grateful to her.
-Call her a sweet nickname.	-Say "I Love you" an awful lot!

    3.) Give Her Your Undivided Attention:

-Make eye contact.	-Don't talk to her & read the paper.
-Show interest in her day.	-Hold her hand and touch her.
-Talk to her about your day.	-Regularly play together.
-Watch her undress.	-Spend an entire day with her.

4.) Serve Her and Share Responsibilities:
- -Make a menu together.
- -Help with laundry/dishes.
- -Put lotion on her feet/legs.
- -Check on sounds at night.
- -Put gas in her car.
- -Help with children.
- -Let her sleep late.
- -Make a budget together.

5.) Physically Adore, Honor, and Love Her:
- -Greet her with a kiss.
- -Give her a massage.
- -Comfort her.
- -Always hug for 7 seconds.
- -Learn to please her sexually.
- -Scratch her back.

6.) Shower Her with Gifts:
- -Encourage her hobby.
- -Send her flowers.
- -Hire outside cleaning help.
- -Be creative and buy a gift.
- -Treat her to a massage.
- -Send her away for a retreat.

7.) "Just Because" You Love Her:
- -Put the toilet seat down.
- -Learn to fight fair.
- -Don't annoy her.
- -Don't reveal secrets.
- -Walk at her pace.
- -Go to bed together.

IV. Ways to Show Love to Your Husband (by love language)

1.) Create and Continually Enhance Meaning and Value for Him:
- -Don't be too critical.
- -Encourage humor.
- -Show value to his friends.
- -Celebrate with him.
- -Discover his favorites.
- -Create a Marriage Covenant.

2.) Encourage, Affirm, and Support Him with Your Words:
- -Praise him with your words.
- -Leave unexpected notes.
- -Appreciate his work.
- -Respect him.
- -Be gentle but honest with him.
- -Speak positively of him in public.

3.) Spend Time with Him:
- -Do things he likes.
- -Enjoy his interests.
- -Set aside date night.
- -Allow him to cry.
- -Teach by example.
- -Have family time together.

4.) Serve Him in the Home:
- Be flexible.
- Share meal responsibilities.
- Cook his favorite meal.
- Don't gripe too much at him.
- Share financial responsibilities.
- Agree on major decisions.

5.) Physically Adore, Honor, and Love Him:
- Learn to hug 7 seconds.
- Initiate intimacy.
- Slow down and be inventive.
- Show him your attention.
- Plan time alone.
- Wear his favorite negligee.
- Say yes more than no.
- Take a bath together.

6.) Give Him Gifts of Love, Time, and Concern:
- Make a list of wants/needs.
- Buy him gifts he likes.
- Attend a marriage workshop.
- Allow him to have quiet time.

7.) "Just Because" You Love Him:
- Allow him a hobby.
- Wear what he likes.
- Let him speak for himself.
- Seek to please him.
- Learn his love language.
- Trust and respect him.

V. Remember these timeless treasures:
- Never say anything that you don't mean!
- Be romantic! Continually date each other!
- In marriage, you can either be happy or be right.
- Three things: 1) Forgive, 2) Forgive, and 3) Forgive.
- Learn the differences between men and women.
- Don't try to change each other.
- Learn each other's needs (emotional, physical, social, and spiritual).
- Remove obstacles to communication.
- Listen to each other attentively and empathetically.
- Genuinely become other-oriented (not selfish!).

VI. Rewrite your marriage vows and hang them prominently in your home! Do this every five years or so. When developing your Marriage Statement, make sure it is your own statement. It can be copied

from other documents, but make sure it is something you both believe as you write it together. Here is a sample Marriage Statement:

We promise to love, honor, and respect each other, to support and uplift each other, trying always to encourage and never to discourage the other. We promise to be honest in gentle and respectful ways and to not be sarcastic, cutting, or angry.

We desire for our love to be a model and will deem the other partner as more important than ourselves. We will strive to love each other unconditionally and to base our love on important values we share. We promise always to forgive each other. We promise to take care of each other in times of stress, sickness, or injury. We promise to raise our children by living lives of example before them.

Realizing that a three-strand cord is not easily broken, we covenant together to commit our lives to each other realizing that love is a decision now and every day for the rest of our lives. We make the decision today and forever to love each other, be committed to each other, learn to communicate with each other, seek to resolve conflict, and faithfully care for each other from this day forward.

VII. Learn personal details about each other's sizes, favorites, dates, etc. Make a list of things you would like to know about your mate. Consider gathering a variety of information you want to know such as his/her favorite meal at specific restaurants, names, anniversaries, birth dates of favorite relatives, sizes of clothing, colors, etc. Exchange lists with your mate, fill the lists out, and talk through the responses. Get to know each other and then utilize the information to show love and honor to one another.

Additional Suggested Resources:
Chapman, Gary. *The Five Love Languages.*
Gray, John. *Men are From Mars, Women are From Venus.*
Harley, Willard F. *His Needs, Her Needs.*
Smalley, Gary. *Making Love Last Forever.*
Rainey, Dennis and Barbara. *Building Your Mate's Self-Esteem.*

Chapter IV.
Roofing for Maximum Protection–Self-Esteem

After laying a solid foundation and building the walls, the next step in building a home is to put on the roof. Like the walls, the roof keeps out the harsh elements. You could spend hundreds of thousands of dollars on the rest of your home, but without a roof that keeps out the rain, snow, and the extreme temperatures, your home would be useless. Establishing identity and building self-worth and self-esteem provides children maximum protection against the unbelievable pressures they face in today's society.

The importance of self-worth and self-esteem simply can't be overstated. A teenager, guy or girl, who feels good about himself or herself for the right reasons, will be able to deal with the pressures of the society we live in. The greatest gift you can give your kids is a self-worth and self-esteem based on the right stuff. As I walk the halls of schools and mix with students in stadiums, I see teenagers pressuring one another. The pressures today and the high stakes of compromise are unbelievably dangerous. Most parents I work with need to realize and acknowledge that their kids are living in a more pressure packed and dangerous world than the one they grew up in. Not only are the pressures greater, they start earlier. My daughter came home with stuff in the seventh grade that I didn't hear until I was a freshman in high school.

You would not believe what some children are dealing with. Several years ago, I was in a small town where just a few weeks earlier a sixth grade boy and his young sixth grade girlfriend had gone over to this young girl's house where they planned to give up their virginity together on a Friday afternoon.

The little boy got nervous and couldn't perform so they stopped. She didn't blab it to everybody in the school; she just told a few of her friends, who told a few of their friends and by Tuesday of the next week, he was the laughing stock of the entire middle school. You see, middle school kids talk about that kind of stuff and they pressure one another. By Thursday morning, he was tired of being made fun of so he went out to catch his bus to school, waited for the bus to leave, and then went back home after both of his parents had gone to work. He got into his dad's night stand, pulled out the 38-caliber pistol, and tragically ended his own life.

Why? Because kids talk about that kind of stuff and the social pressure they put on each other is incredible.

A young girl walked up to me at a high school assembly in Texas. She said, "Where were you when I needed you? I'm fourteen years old and I'm already pregnant." That night, she came to the conference and decided to start making winning choices. Her story is more common than most of us would like to admit.

It was her ninth grade year; she was gorgeous, popular, and a cheer-leader but had not dated much. There were too many guys in her school who wanted to date girls who would put out–yet they wanted to marry one that never had. Her values

> ## *The pressure comes earlier and is greater than it has ever been.*

were such that she wanted her husband to be the first and only one to know her sexually. Further, she wanted it to be after they got married. So, she didn't play the game. The beginning of her sophomore year, she started dating the fullback of the football team. They spent a lot of time together and had a great relationship. He said that he agreed with her values and he was different. For a while, he was different. But then he began to manipulate her, "If you love me, you'll let me. If you love me, you'll produce. Come on, everybody else is doing it." It was either let him or lose him. She blew off her values because she wanted to be accepted.

That's exactly where kids are today. Unless there is a sense of identity, self-worth, and self-esteem based on the right stuff, they are going to compromise. We must understand how important pressure from the group is, and make sure our students are grounded in the right stuff.

How do we establish identity and build self-worth and self-esteem? There are three key principles:

First, we must model a healthy, growing, marriage relationship. If you're single, take courage. You can do the next best thing, which is to become a healthy, growing individual. You can become the winner that you dream to be and your kids will find a tremendous amount of security. I would encourage you to do something else. Find a same sex mentor for your child who can help build positive characteristics into their lives and model for them. If you are married, the idea is to model a healthy, growing marriage relationship. Children and youth find a tremendous amount of security in the love relationship between mom and dad.

While a healthy intimate marriage was the subject of the last chapter, let me mention one additional thought here. This is a major commitment that must be made without condition. Never, ever, ever stop dating. Most marriages get in

> ### *Where are we as a couple?*

trouble because the couple stops doing the basic things that led them to grow into love and get married in the first place. My daughter was nine days old the first time a babysitter came to take care of her so that her mom and I could go on a date. Every month we go on a major date even if we can only afford to split an order of fries at McDonald's and go to a dollar movie. Then, at least once a year, and most of the time twice a year, we take a long weekend away from our two children. My kids have rarely seen my wife get in the car when I have not opened the door for her. The point is this: we continue to do the things that led us to grow into love and get married in the first place.

If you want to affair-proof your marriage and provide an atmosphere of love and security for your children, then work at cultivating those sources of security in your marriage. If you don't, your marriage will grow cold and everyone will suffer.

> ### *Tell your wife that she looks pretty even if she looks like a truck. —Ricky, age 7*

The second thing we must do in order to establish identity and build self-worth and self-esteem is to point our children in the right direction. There are basically only two directions–the wrong direction and the right direction.

The wrong direction can be summed up in one word: external. In other words, the stuff on the outside that has come to be the symbols of success. What are the symbols of success in our society? We used to call these the three B's–beauty, brains, and bucks. What are the things that a student has to have these days in order to be deemed successful? For a guy, he needs to drive the right kind of car. Over the years, I have discovered guys can be driving an $800 truck, but if it has $1,000 wheels and a $2,000 stereo system it's still okay. Girls, on the other hand, seem to be more concerned over a relationship with a person of the opposite sex than any other single thing. I have seen more young ladies sacrifice their values over this issue than all others combined. Other symbols of success, of course, include things like wearing the right labels, achieving popularity, and being successful in sports.

The symbols of success in our culture are the external things. Is there anything wrong with any of these things? Is it wrong to be dated? Wrong to have a nice car? Wrong to be popular? No, there's nothing wrong with any of those symbols of success except they are temporary. They can and often do change very rapidly. The external symbols are a poor place to look for your self-worth and your self-esteem.

The right direction is the internal stuff–the stuff on the inside. In order for a young person to have healthy self-worth and self-esteem, it must be based upon that which does not change–the real person on the inside. A young person's character must be based on the enduring values of honesty, integrity, and truthfulness. It's the essence of who you are when you're lying in bed alone. Who you are at the very core of your person is what counts. Not what you **do**–the behavior–which is external. Rather, who you are. It means, "I am a special person of worth." I once overheard a student respond incredibly to being pressured to compromise her values. She said, "I don't care what you think of me, I'm a special person of worth created in the image of God for His special purpose and plan. And God doesn't make junk."

If you come from a religious frame of reference, please take a cue from this young lady. A person's faith perspective has everything to do with this vital area. Once students have decided their core values and have established a clear portrait of the person they want to become, they are

> *When a brave man takes a stand, the spines of others are stiffened. —Billy Graham*

much better equipped to deal with the incredible pressure of today's world.

How do you point them in the right direction? There are two practical things you can do.

First, you can help them by modeling appropriate behavior and choices. Students learn through seeing someone they care about become before them what, in their hearts, they really want to be. We will look at this exhaustively in the next section.

Second, we point them in the right direction through helping them set their priorities. All over the world, it's the same. It doesn't make any difference whether it is in Europe, South America, Australia, or Hong Kong. For some reason the world over, parents tell their kids that it is what's on the inside that really matters, and yet they push their kids to excel through the external symbols of success.

I watch parents push their kids academically, push them socially, and live their dreams through them athletically. Yet parents have not really thought through the issues of purpose in life, core values, character development, and helping their children to develop a personal growth plan. What messages are parents giving their children when they focus on the external? The message is that being the winner is not about what you are on the inside; it's about excelling in this sport or that academic contest.

Let me illustrate how the message of what's really important is often lost through setting priorities. Several summers ago, I was invited to do an event for an organization in Mississippi. They wanted me to speak to about 300 students on developing a personal growth plan. In order to build attendance, they asked me to do a sign-up rally four weeks in advance. Twenty-two eighth grade boys signed up, but only three actually attended the event. Why? Several weeks previous, the basketball coach in the private school where all of these kids attended decided he was going to hold a basketball camp the first week of June. Do you know how many of the boys who actually went to the basketball camp really wanted to go? None of them. They went to basketball camp because their dads made them go.

A large group of parents could have gone to the coach and said, "Listen, this event has been planned for two years, and our kids are going there rather than to the basketball camp." But not only did the parents not do that, they sat down with their boys and said, "Realistically if you don't go to camp you're not going to play next year." By the way, there is no difference between saying to your son, "Realistically if you don't go to camp you are not going to play" and saying to your daughter, "If you don't put out, you're not going to be dated." If the second statement bothers you, the first statement ought to bother you, too.

Through setting priorities we must communicate that our self-worth is not based on what we do or how we perform but on who we are on the inside. Our students need to learn from our example and by watching us set priorities that we believe success is truly an inside job!

The third way we establish identity and build self-worth and self-esteem is this. . . we love our children unconditionally. This is where we shower our kids with unconditional love and acceptance.

> ## *Love children unconditionally.*

This sounds so easy. Why do we have such a hard time with unconditional love and acceptance? Three reasons:

First, the performance syndrome–this is where we use our love and acceptance as an incentive like a carrot to motivate our children to be their best. In other words, if they do well on their report card, in sports, and the other things we want them to do, then we shower them with love and acceptance. If they don't, we use our love and acceptance as a carrot. Many parents withhold unconditional love and acceptance when they know their kids are doing less than they are capable of because they are afraid of rewarding that negative behavior. So they keep it out of reach. But here is the danger. They end up with self-worth and self-esteem based on performance–and that is very dangerous.

If students learn that they have to perform for you in order to receive your love and acceptance, then they will not only perform for you, but they'll perform for their friends as well. Just think about how potentially dangerous that could be.

Let's say Johnny comes home with straight A's and we say, "Johnny you made straight A's on your report card; I am so proud of you." What is that? It's performance-based affirmation. As a parent, what is the message we're giving? We're saying, "If he hadn't made straight A's, I wouldn't be proud of him." So how can you reward that report card and stress personhood? You could say, "Johnny, I am so excited that learning is important to you." See the difference?

Personhood not performance. Unconditional love and acceptance must be based upon just their personhood. If you were to walk up to my children, Paige and Josh, and ask either one what they would have to do to make their mom and dad proud of them, they would respond, "Nothing, they're proud just because I am Paige and just because I'm Josh." (We started when they were one, two, three years of age.) Every day of their life, we walk up to them, grab them by the ears, and we say, "Paige and Josh I love you, I'm proud of you, you are so awesome. Do you know why I'm proud of you?" Of course when they were two and three, they had no clue–but we would say, "We are proud of you just because you're Paige and just because you're Josh." Please start today showering your children with unconditional love and acceptance. It is never too late.

I was in Scotland a few years ago and met a young lady on a train. In the conversation, I was talking to this girl and her friend, and mentioned the love and acceptance message I share daily with Paige. Tears came to her eyes as she said this to me, "I'd give anything if I could hear my daddy say that just once." Shower them with unconditional love and acceptance.

Every child, every teenager has an emotional fuel tank. What we need to do is keep that emotional fuel tank full to overflowing with unconditional love and acceptance. However, many of us struggle with loving unconditionally.

The first reason we struggle with unconditional love and acceptance is performance. **Second, we struggle with issues of preference or personal favoritism.** If you have more than one child, it is easy to have a favorite. I used to think any mom or dad who would favor one child over another would have to be a totally disgusting parent and the reason I felt that way is because my dad loved my older brother more than he loved me. My older brother was the apple of his eye. He was the first born son.

When I was in my late twenties, my dad and I talked and joked about this issue. He admitted that my perception was correct. My dad was surprised that it was so obvious during our growing up years.

Several years ago, I observed a perfect example of why parents sometimes have favorites. This lady had two boys. Alex had blonde hair, blue eyes, and was unbelievably cute. He had a compliant personality and just wanted to please you. He was so easy to be around even during the years of seven to ten, when boys have so much energy and can easily get on your last nerve; he was fun to be around. They had a second child whose name was John and this guy gave strong-willed a brand-new perspective. If you waited ten years and looked up the definition of strong-willed, you would see John's picture. I saw his

> ### *Parents of teens know why some animals eat their young.*

dad give him a spanking once that bordered on child abuse. Afterward, John looked into his dad's eyes and said, "I am **NOT** crying" and he didn't. As a middle-schooler, John was diagnosed with hyperactivity and ADD. If you didn't have a little easier time around Alex than John, you would need a psychological examination. There are just some kids that are easier to like.

My wife struggles with impatience because when she looks at my daughter, she sees herself in the mirror. They have identical personalities and therefore, they are like oil and water. But she has infinite patience with my son. If you have multiple children, it's easy to have favorites but we must guard against preference.

The third is perfectionism. If you struggle with perfectionism, and even if you don't, I want to encourage you to do this activity. Set up a ledger for every relationship in your house. Your spouse, children, grandchildren, every-

> ### *Give children 7 to 1 positive comments.*

one–set up a ledger. On one side, write all of your positive comments and on the other, write all of your negative comments. While you're thinking about your negative comments, think about this: There is no such thing as constructive criticism. Criticism is criticism. I don't care how positively you state the criticism.

My dad used to talk about buttering the bread; you build somebody up and then you tell them what they probably don't want to hear. Then, you encourage them again. My dad's suggestion on sharing constructive criticism was a good one. When it is necessary, I follow his advice. However, the point is, regardless of how positively you share it, criticism is criticism.

Your comments to your kids need to be at least seven to one in the positive. For every comment that is negative, you need to be creative and say seven positive things to them.

The best management principle I know is this, "What gets rewarded gets done." With your teenagers, try and catch them doing something right and brag on them. Make a note every time you see them doing something right and brag on them. Walk up to your children, grab them by the ears and say, "I love you. You are awesome. I can't wait to see what you do with your life."

For example, my wife and I right now are trying to help our children learn how to sit down at a table and eat like human beings. We're not asking for a lot; we just want them to be able to sit down at a table and eat like humans. We have promised each other that we are not going to waste one ounce of negative energy over teaching them how to eat. We try to

> *One compliment can keep me going for a whole month.*
> *—Mark Twain*

wait until the first time in the meal we catch them doing something right, then tell them "Great! You are chewing with your mouth closed; that is awesome! We haven't reminded you to chew with your mouth closed once and you are doing it because you want to. I'm glad that's important to you."

If you constantly look to find your kids doing something wrong, you'll spend every moment of every day correcting them. Is that not true? But, what gets rewarded gets done.

Just try to rethink that. With an adolescent if you spend your time nitpicking, you will destroy their self-worth and their self-esteem trying to achieve perfection. It's a mistake to do that! Try to catch them doing something right and brag on them.

Three ways to love unconditionally

How do you love unconditionally? There are three primary ways.

First, share your love verbally. Say it out loud. I'm not an emotional person...I almost have to write it on my DayTimer to do this every day. On the other hand, my wife is an emotional person so this comes more naturally for her. Regardless of our emotional make-up, we must verbally work on filling the emotional fuel tanks of our kids.

There is a great story about a man who had not said to his wife in fifty years, the words "I love you." Here was his rationale, "When I married her fifty years ago, I told her that I loved her; if I ever change my mind, I'll let her know."

That doesn't work.

Your children, your grandchildren, your spouse, these people need to constantly hear verbally, "I love you."

Second, don't just say it–say it with meaning. Say it with feeling. Fill your speech with value and acceptance. There was a great football player who played in the National Football League. He had two sons who were also football players...linemen...big guys. They were in a wedding and were walking down the sidewalk wearing red tuxedos with pink satin lapels. They also had on white ruffled shirts with pink satin ties, and white patent-leather shoes. Remember, they were linemen. They were not feeling very good about their appearance. As they were walking down the sidewalk, their shoulders were slumped forward. They were probably thinking "I hope that nobody I know sees me in this outfit."

The dad, seeing his two sons walking down the sidewalk, could tell they were probably in need of encouragement. He walked up and said, "You look sensational; you look absolutely incredible! In fact, when the wedding is over, don't take these tuxes back; buy them. You just look great!"

You know what happened? The two sons followed him around the rest of the evening because he

> *Dear God: I bet it is very hard for You to love everybody in the whole world. There are only four people in our family and I can never do it. —Nan, age 4*

was the only person who said something encouraging. Don't just say it; fill your speech with value and acceptance toward your spouse, your children, and other important people around you. People know the difference.

Third, say it when they blow it. Share unconditional love when they least deserve it.

My father taught me this principle of saying it when it is least deserved. I grew up as a rebellious teenager. It was always legal in our house to drink as long as you didn't abuse alcohol or drink and drive. Drinking and driving was

> ## *Give them your love when they least deserve it.*

definitely against the rules. One night, I drove home plastered. As I pulled into the driveway, my mom and dad's light was on. I don't know if you have ever had your whole life pass right before your eyes, but that happened for me as I pulled into the driveway.

I knew that I was dead.

My dad had been a Sergeant in the Marines. You never asked him, "Why" questions unless you were willing to peel your face off the wall on the other side of the room. I am grateful for a lot of things that I learned from my dad–he taught me about discipline. But he was a Marine at heart–he was very tough.

As I walked into the house, I will never forget what happened next; my dad was standing there in his boxer shorts and was extremely angry until he saw the condition I was in. Until that moment, I had never, in my life, seen my dad cry. But that night, my dad began to weep, and he said, "Jerry, I am so glad you're home. I love you. I am so proud of you." He helped me get undressed, he put me to bed, he kissed me on the forehead, and said, "Jerry, I love you. I am so grateful you're home."

As he turned out the light and walked down the hall, I thought to myself, "I have driven up to the wrong house." The next morning the conversation started with, "I love you and I'm proud of you." I don't remember the price I paid for that mistake (only that it was stiff); what I remember is that my dad showered me with unconditional love based on who I was.

It is very hard to do that–but before you say to your kids, "Your momma brought you into this world; I'm taking you out," shower them with unconditional love.

The greatest gift you can give to your children is self-worth and self-esteem based on the right stuff. Remember, success is an inside job. You would never live in a home without a roof to protect your family from the elements. Your kids need the same protection from a pressure-packed and dangerous world.

> **The best place to be when you are sad is in Grandpa's lap.**

Put on Your Construction Hat and Let's Go to Work!

Consulting the Blueprint

What concepts from this chapter can I work on, learn, or practice?

These concepts will increase the value of my family in what ways?

What can I do to apply these principles in a practical way?

Building Blocks for My Home

With concepts from this chapter, what are practical steps I can take to build my family and create a "healthier" home?

One:

Two:

Three:

Basic Blocks For Building

I. Some ideas and suggestions for improving the self-esteem of your spouse, your children, and your family in general:

For Spouse
- Listen attentively and empathetically, making eye contact.
- Talk, listen, and share your life.
- Learn to communicate, listen, and resolve conflict.
- Have a consistent "date" with each other.
- Spend time getting to know each other's favorites and other important information.
- Provide safety and security in your home.
- Accentuate the positive–always look for the positive.

For Children
- Demonstrate unconditional love.
- Spend quality and quantity time with them.
- Compliment them, brag on them, and show "pride" in them.
- Show consistent interest in their school.
- Give yourself to them often on their turf.
- Say "I Love You!" a lot with your words, with notes, and actions.
- Create an atmosphere where children feel free to ask questions and feel comfortable exploring answers.
- Get to know your child.

II. Some VERY important Do's and Don'ts of Marriage:

Do's
- Commit to your spouse for life–unconditionally.
- Seek to understand before being understood.
- Be transparent and open to your spouse.
- Always make eye contact when you talk to your spouse.
- Learn to resolve conflict in healthy ways.
- Touch your spouse a lot–cherish them!
- Learn to say the following often: "I love you." "I'm sorry." "I made a mistake." "Please forgive me." "I forgive you."

-Constantly speak positive affirmations.
-Support each other–especially in public.
-Practice patience with each other.

Don'ts
-Don't attack character–only address behavior.
-Don't keep track of past offenses.
-Don't touch each other in anger!
-Don't say, "You should," or "You shouldn't."
-Don't use the "D" word in a threat–or at all! (Divorce).
-Don't say anything that you don't mean.
-Don't go to bed with unresolved anger.
-Don't ever compare each other to anyone in a negative way.

Additional Suggested Resources:
Dobson, James. *Preparing for Adolescence.*
Chapman, Gary and Ross Campbell. *The Five Love Languages for Children.*
Clarke, Jean Illsley. *Self-Esteem: A Family Affair.*
Smalley, Gary and John Trent. *The Blessing.*
Ziglar, Zig. *Raising Positive Kids in a Negative World.*

Chapter V.
Wiring for Sound–Communication

We live in an information age. Today's children have no idea what life is like without computers. Not long ago, my son Josh was complaining about being sick. Debra checked for a fever and found none. She told Josh he probably had a virus. He was offended and said, "Mom, I'm not a computer."

The next step in building your house is to wire it for sound. That includes wiring for entertainment, phone communication, and the internet. Healthy families must do the same through building bridges of communication in the home.

You say I love you to a spouse, child, or a teenager with four letters: T-I-M-E. You cannot buy them with clothes, cars, or stuff. Children are masters of manipulation and they will try to get you to believe that you can buy them with those things. But, you cannot buy them; the only way

> *Children will soon forget your presents. They will always remember your presence.*

you can say I love you and make it mean something to them is by giving yourself to them on their turf.

Please understand this distinction. When you give yourself to them on their turf–doing what you and they both know you're doing just for them, it means something to them.

Parents often live their lives through their children. My dad did that with my brother and me through football. He never, ever, ever, missed a football game. My dad was absolutely, passionately committed to two things: his lake house and our football. About the only times I saw my dad as a teenager was at the lake house and when I laced up my shoes and looked up in the stands at a football game.

However, more than football, I loved tennis and track. My dad never saw me play in a tennis tournament and he never saw me run in a track meet. My dad did not care about track. He didn't care about tennis. He cared about football and his lake house.

As adults my dad and I have had a great relationship and I don't question his love for me when I was a teenager. However, please read this principle carefully: It is not what you feel for your kids that matters–it's what you communicate and what you communicate is what you communicate by giving yourself on their turf. I was probably twenty-five years old before I realized how much my dad loved me. The point is that from about twelve to age twenty-five I could have known that. You say I love you by giving yourself to your children on their turf, by doing something they, and you know, you are doing just for them.

I take my daughter out on a date every month. It's a daddy-daughter date. I've been doing it since she was about seven or eight years of age. My daughter is like my wife in that she likes to shop. Here's the rule on our dates: She is the boss, so she chooses the restaurant and whatever she wants to do after that...she's the boss. Do you know what she chooses about three or four times a year? You got it–shopping. I would rather spend three hours in a steam room with the Village People than go shopping. When I need something at the mall, I park as close to where I'm going in as possible. I rush in, go straight to the store, make the purchase, and I'm out of there in ten minutes.

When I take my daughter to the mall, it's not the purchase that counts; it's the pursuit of the purchase that matters. We usually end up buying something in two and a half hours that we could have bought in the first ten minutes. The fact that I would walk around the mall for two and a half to three hours, holding her hand, talking, laughing, and having a great time means the world to my daughter. A parent says "I love you" to their child by spending time with them on their turf.

One of the most important parts of communication is learning effective ways to listen. **There are five levels of listening.** I included these briefly in an earlier chapter but here is a more detailed explanation.

The first one is ignoring. You're not listening and not even trying to communicate you are listening. You are simply ignoring the speaker. You might think, "Now wait a minute, nobody would do that on purpose–nobody who cares about their wife, their kids, their husband."

We do this almost without realizing it though. It is very possible for me to be at home and be a million miles away. I am passionate about what I do. And I've learned that it's possible for me to come home and be there physically and, at the same time, be a million miles away emotionally and intellectually.

> ## *Listen to the whispers and you won't have to hear the screams.*
> ## *—Cherokee Saying*

In recent years when I get about two miles from my house, I refocus my attention to my family. I mentally lay aside the unresolved issues related to business and focus on what I sense to be Debra, Paige, and Josh's needs. For the last several miles of my trip home, I focus on my role as a husband and father. This process has made a difference in really being home on all levels.

The second level is pretend listening. This is where you're trying to communicate that you're listening, but you're not. I like to unwind by catching thirty minutes of news. Just one uninterrupted session of *Headline News* does wonders in helping me unwind and find out what happened in the world during the day. I have to read so much in my business that I don't really want to read the paper to find out what happened to the world, so thirty minutes of *Headline News* and I am a happy camper. Almost always, during this thirty minute segment, my wife or one of my children have to solve a problem. If I don't focus on them but rather continue trying to do what I'm doing, they may feel like the next time they will find someone else who really cares.

Or mom, you have fifteen pots and pans going and, of course, if you stop, no one is going to eat. It's at that moment someone needs to solve a problem. So you try to tune in to them and do your thing, and they get that feeling like nobody cares. At least stop, look them in the eye and say, "After we eat we'll go somewhere, have something to drink, and it'll be just you and me, together for a while."

The third level of listening is selective listening. This is what we do with people who talk a lot. Do you have people in your life who talk a lot? Moms, this is what you do with your preschoolers. Preschoolers have this constant running chatter-thing going. From the time they get up until the time they go to bed, they're talking all the time.

My son Josh talks all the time. I took him on an eight-day speaking tour of New England when he was four and a half years old. Just me and Josh. I found out that from the time he got up until the time he went to bed, he talked–sometimes fourteen hours a day. Additionally, I discovered that every toy he owns has a name and if he wasn't talking to me, he was talking to one of them. When he wasn't talking to them, he was talking to himself.

One day my administrative assistant called and said, "Jerry, I need you to take care of some issues. Do them on your computer, send them back to me by e-mail, and I'll take care of it for you." I said, "Josh, I am not going to be able to play with you this afternoon so you need to entertain yourself." He did great for about two and a half hours. He got bored and started to talk to me, but I wasn't listening. I was in my own world. Finally, when he was tired of being ignored, he pulled on my pants legs and after he had gotten my attention, he crossed his little arms and said, "Daddy, when I talk to you, would you please look at me?" I think he'd heard that before.

The fourth level is attentive listening. This means you're attending. You are genuinely tuned in, and you're listening to what someone has to say. You're actively listening for content; you're trying to hear what they have to say.

The fifth and most powerful level of listening is empathetic listening. This is where you are empathizing. You are really trying to tune in to what a person is saying–not just what they're saying, but the emotion behind it. You listen for content with your ears, but you listen for emotion with your eyes. You're listening for anger, frustration, disappointment, etc. As you listen empathetically, you reflect back the emotion that you see. It's like unpeeling an onion; you're trying to get to the soft inner core of what they really want to tell you. Most of the time when teenagers or adults speak to you, what they start speaking about is not really what they want to talk about. Empathetic listening is getting to what they really want to talk about, that soft inner core. It often sounds like, "I can see that made you angry." Empathy is not sympathy. You're not necessarily agreeing with what they're saying, but you're just reflecting back the emotion. The one speaking feels deeply understood. Stephen Covey is right, "The key to personal influence is to first be influenced." When people know that you feel what they feel and can relate to their pain, they want to hear what you have to say.

Our problem in communicating is that while people are talking to us, what we're thinking about is what we're going to say next. Have you ever said, "Oh yeah, I can relate to that. One time. . ." You think you're communicating and they're frustrated because you're not connecting.

Three listening mistakes

In addition to the five levels of listening, there are three listening mistakes that you need to be aware of and avoid as a spouse and/or a parent.

The three listening mistakes are first, "pretend" listening. People need to know when they talk to you that they are your focus. You say "I love you" by giving of yourself. So if you're watching television, trying to read the paper, cooking a meal, and at the same time you're trying to connect with your child, grandchild, or your spouse, it's not going to work.

Have you ever talked to someone who didn't make eye contact with you? I used to work with a person who never looked where he talked. This guy could be awesome if we could just get him to talk and look at the same place.

The second listening mistake is "One Up" listening. Parents are great at this one. I got sick and tired of hearing how difficult it was to "walk to school fifteen miles through the wind, rain, and snow, uphill both directions with no shoes on." When Josh was a newborn, I discovered that parents don't get better at this when they get older. Josh, when he was born, suffered from severe colic. We just could not get him to sleep. The doctors didn't seem to care if Josh was sleeping or not. They prescribed Mylicon drops which were useless. Then they gave us some unbelievably insightful suggestions like, "Why don't you hold your baby over the dryer?" or "Take him for a drive at bedtime." Of course, you know none of that worked. After about three or four nights of not sleeping, we asked, "Doc, we really need some help; what about a prescription of Paragoric?" He responded, "WE DO NOT GIVE OPIUM TO CHILDREN!" Never mind that my mom gave it to all four of us when we were kids and none of us are heroin addicts. I was fortunate enough that I had a doctor friend that I went to high school with; I called him up and he helped us with a prescription. We gave Josh just a couple of drops a night for a week and I'm happy to say at ten, he's not a heroin addict. And we were able to start getting some sleep.

During the course of this ordeal, I called my mom on the telephone, "Mom, how are you doing?" She said, "I'm doing fine, how are you doing?" I said, "Well, I'm a little tired since I haven't slept in two weeks–Josh has been up with colic." Mom said, "Oh that's no big deal; we had four of you and all of you had colic at the same time." (That was seriously hard to believe since the four of us were spread out over seven years.)

I want you to know that when our kids are struggling, they don't care to hear how difficult it was when we were kids. Telling them things like this is a wonderful way to eliminate communication altogether. When your friend at work is struggling, and you respond by saying, "Oh, I can relate to that." Then, you begin to talk about your war stories, you may think you're communicating, but when they are hurting, they don't care about your previous difficulties. It's a sure way to eliminate communication with the people you want to connect with. Reading our home movies into their lives is not what they're looking for.

The third listening mistake is "Barney Fife" listening. Do you remember Barney? Andy only gave him one bullet. Barney was always trying to "nip it...nip it in the bud." This is something most parents struggle with especially with their kids or grandkids. They begin to talk about a problem and potential solution. Instead of listening and steering them through it, we immediately cut them off and give them a "three points and a poem" lecture on why their proposed course of action is not the best. Remember, you should never, ever, ever, ever, tell a middle school or high school student anything you can lead them to discover for themselves.

Remember, begin with the end in mind. What are we trying to accomplish long term with our kids? We're trying to help them leave our house by age eighteen having decided for themselves they want to be the best they can be. We're trying to help them learn how to make life choices. You can't help them learn how to make life choices by telling them what to do every time they get into a difficult situation. So, what we need to do first, is let them know we love them enough to listen to everything they've got to say. We need to let them pour it out. Most of the time, kids will solve their own problems if we allow them to talk and think them through. So, we need to love them enough to listen to what they've got to say. Second, we try to help them solve their problems by asking the right questions. I'm not saying you should never share your Barney Fife silver bullet lecture, but it ought to be the last choice, not the first response.

There are four hints on listening for understanding.

The first one is reflecting back feelings. Get the people you love and care about to talk about what they feel. Listen with your eyes for what they feel. Remember, you listen for content with your ears, but you listen for emotion with your eyes. Don't play the fifty questions game. In the business world, this is called probing.

Let me tell you a little bit about my wife. My wife and I are so fundamentally different. She is a detail person; I'm a dreamer. I see the big picture and dream the dream. Debra sees the sixty-nine reasons why the dream is not very realistic; it's wonderful we are on the same team together because we're a good fit. In terms of communication, our differences make the process interesting. In the early years of our marriage, I would come home trying to be a good husband, trying to get my wife involved in my day. I would be twenty-five minutes into what should have been maybe a five or six minute story; at this point, I had been interrupted sixty-nine times because I wasn't giving enough information. I'm twenty-five minutes into a six minute story and I'm frustrated–I don't even want to tell the rest of the stupid story.

My wife and I have both compromised. My wife knows that I'm trying to be sensitive to give more details. On the other side, she's letting me share the story the way I want to share it. She no longer plays the fifty questions game and I try to be sensitive to her need for more information. By probing and asking questions, you may think you're communicating how much you're interested, but it's really very manipulative. It puts you in control of the conversation instead of them. Listen, without interruption, and as you see anger or frustration, reflect back what you see. For example, you could say, "I know that had to be frustrating." Reflect back the feelings you see in them very gently.

The second hint is to determine their perspective. If there is a problem to be solved, make sure you understand it by repeating it briefly and asking for clarification. For example, "This is what I understand that you're struggling with; is this right?" If you are not careful, you could end up spending a whole lot of time trying to answer a question that they're really not asking. Make sure to determine their perspective. Many times a friend or family member will just want to share an experience and they just want you to listen–there's nothing more to be done.

Third, ask good leading questions. Good leading questions are questions that are open-ended. For example, if you're trying to solve a problem, you might ask a question like, "What are your options?" Let them come up with whatever they think the options may be. Good leading questions are open-ended and they become more and more specific as you narrow in on a solution.

The fourth hint is to give your loved ones room. I realize this sounds contradictory. The first hint was to encourage the expression of feelings. This is empathetic listening–reflecting back the emotion you see. Don't go beyond reflecting back what you see in an attempt to push someone to talk about the really painful things going on inside of them. If you try to force them to do that, they'll lock you out. I mentioned earlier that I take my daughter on a monthly date. Paige usually chooses a nice restaurant that will ensure a long evening. That's great for me because I want a lot of time with her. Normally, during the time we are together, she controls the conversation talking about her friends and the events they're involved in. As she has gotten older, maybe two or three times a year (and we have a great relationship), she opens up about something that is really painful in her life.

I need to drop a statement in right here for those who are parenting preschoolers and elementary children. I want this statement to be sobering, but don't allow it to scare you. Good communication with an elementary-ager will become strained in adolescence. Poor communication will be eliminated. Capture these early years to wire your home for sound. Take advantage of this time–because when your children become teenagers, you'll be glad you did. If you have teenagers and your communication is poor–don't give up. Apply the principles of this chapter; it will take time and will not be easy, but it will be well worth the effort. Happy wiring!

Put on Your Construction Hat and Let's Go to Work!

Consulting the Blueprint
What concepts from this chapter can I work on, learn, or practice?

These concepts will increase the value of my family in what ways?

What can I do to apply these principles in a practical way?

Building Blocks for My Home
With concepts from this chapter, what are practical steps I can take to build my family and create a "healthier" home?
One:

Two:

Three:

Basic Blocks For Building

Some nuggets of wisdom:
1. Ask good leading questions.
2. Develop your listening skills.
3. Don't allow your television to dominate your home.
4. Be quick to hear, slow to speak, and slow to anger.
5. Seek first to understand, then be understood.
6. Constantly practice forgiveness.
7. Determine the other's perspective.
8. Respect and value the differences between people.
9. Demonstrate unconditional love.
10. Make eye contact when you talk to others.
11. Leave notes, write letters, and show your love consistently.

12. Have family meetings.
13. Utilize a chore chart with children.
14. Play games and have fun as a couple and family.
15. Utilize meal times for building your family.
16. Build trust, openness, and transparency.

Additional Suggested Resources:
Dettoni, John and Carol. *Parenting Before and After Work.*
Brett, Doris. *Annie Stories: A Special Kind of Storytelling.*

Section Three

Maintain and Increase the Value of Your Investment

> **The greatest thing in family life is to take a hint when a hint is intended and not to take a hint when a hint isn't intended.**
> **—Robert Frost**

Chapter VI.
Adding Insulation—Mentoring Your Children

One of the greatest things you can do to maintain your home and increase the value of your investment is to add insulation. It makes controlling the atmosphere of your home easier. Additional insulation will keep your house warmer in the winter and cooler in the summer while saving you money. The last two homes we sold, the buyer demanded photo-copies of our last twelve month's utility costs. They were checking on our insulation. Most parents I meet and work with are passionate about passing on their core values to their children. They want the best for their children and grandchildren. The transfer of our values is a lot more about the atmosphere in our homes than the actual words we speak. **In this chapter we are going to look at some basic mentoring principles. We want to create an atmosphere in our homes that facilitates passing the really important things in life on to our children.**

The first step in this process is understanding the territory. We are losing our kids primarily during the adolescent years so I will spend most of this discussion focusing on that age group. However, let me make a few observations on each age group.

Preschoolers need two important things. They need to be showered with unconditional love and acceptance because they need the security those two things bring. Second, they need to learn to respond to authority. When you allow a two year old to run your house, you have made a serious mistake. When they ask why, "Because I said so" is fine. They need to learn to respond to your authority, because if they don't, they will struggle with every other authority structure along the way. Eventually, they will have to be broken in adolescence. That can be dangerous—and remember the stakes can be high. So, they need to learn to respond to authority and they need unconditional love and acceptance.

Elementary children think concretely. If you try to speak to them in abstract terms, you will find yourself very, very frustrated. Most people would call these the troublefree years. You may have an extremely strong-willed child and right now you're thinking, "Troublefree, give me a break!" These years are the least challenging for most parents. During this time, shower them with unconditional love and acceptance, wire for sound, and remember they learn and think concretely. Your example is a hundred times more important than your words with your children. Duplicity will be an expensive mistake with this age group.

Teenagers are best described as human beings in transition. They're not children anymore, but neither are they adults. Physically, they're starting to look like adults, but emotionally and psychologically, for the most part, both feet

> **Teenagers are best described as human beings in transition.**

are firmly planted in mid-air. One day, you're amazed at how "with it" your teenager is. You're thinking, "They are really growing up. This is incredible."

Then, the next day, you're completely dumbfounded, "How did this person who was so 'with it' yesterday become so entirely clueless in just twenty-four hours?"

Let me give you two definitions here for your encouragement.

The word "teen" comes from the Latin word, which means "pain, misery, and grief." (Just thought that would encourage you.) Adolescence means "state of destruction." So, whoever thought up these terms knew what it would be like to go through this period in their lives.

We make a very serious mistake when we treat our children like miniature adults. Physically they're beginning to get there, but emotionally and psychologically they're not there. During the first two years of adolescence, the brain of the teenager literally doubles in size. That does not mean that they become twice as intelligent–that is what they think it means. I saw a poster out in Los Angeles that said, "Hire a teenager while he still knows everything."

What it literally means is this: they will begin in this period of their life to question everything. You say it's white; they'll say it's black. The phrase, "You could argue with a signpost" probably originated during this time of life. They are going to question everything! What we must do is create an atmosphere in our homes in which we encourage teens to ask even more questions. You are probably thinking, "I have never had suicidal tendencies; I don't have them right now. Why would I do something that sounds so 'Kentucky-fried' stupid? Why do I want to create more questions?"

Four decisions that every teenager must make

There are four major decisions that every teenager must make for himself or herself before they leave our homes to launch out in life. There are four decisions that they need to nail down under your supervision, or you and your young person are going to be in a world of hurt.

First, teens must decide the key questions of life. The questions like, "Who am I? What is my purpose in life? What about the future?" They need to answer those questions for themselves. You cannot make them choose your values. They have to decide to do that because that is what they want. You may be able to force them into submission while they live in your house, but when they leave your house, they're going to do what they want to do. So, the key is how do you create the right kind of atmosphere in a family? How do you put the right circumstances in place so that it would be natural for them to choose to be the best they can be?

The second question our teens must decide is, "How will my friends impact the way I make life choices?" They must decide how they will deal with the pressure of the group. By the way, this issue is not just a teen one. In fact, students struggle with it because adults do.

How many adults spend money they don't have to live where they can't afford to live, to drive what they can't afford to drive, and to wear what they can't afford to wear, in order to impress people they don't even like? Do you realize that most Americans live no more than a paycheck or two from bankruptcy? Why do Americans live on the edge financially? Because it is important to Americans to have what everybody else has. Most people decided that when they were teenagers.

Third, teens today must decide how they will relate to the opposite sex. The patterns and attitudes they develop as students will impact them tremendously over the rest of their lives. More than eighty-five percent of the students in America believe sex before or outside of marriage is okay. That statistic has remained static for a long time. Of those who have gotten married since 1980, it is estimated that eighty percent will experience the agony of at least one affair. These early attitudes continue to have a huge impact upon their future marriages.

Fourth, teenagers must determine their life values. What is their philosophy of life? What is their worldview? What are their life values?

Teenagers are human beings in transition. They are going to make, unmake, and remake all four of these decisions about 16,000 times during the teenage years. We must provide an atmosphere while they are younger to answer some of these tough questions and be ready to help them make the decisions before they leave our home. They're human beings in transition.

Have you ever seen a student attend an inspirational event or a sports clinic and get pumped up about being a winner or a great athlete? For a while you were amazed at their drive and discipline. However, three weeks later or a few months later, they are back into the same, uninspired rut of settling for less.

They are human beings in transition. They are in the process of making up their mind what they believe about themselves and the world around them, and these decisions will likely change on a regular basis.

Our question must be, in light of this ever shifting territory, "How can we pass on our values? What is really important to the next generation? How do we help our teenagers choose the values that will help them be the best they can be?"

There are three key principles to mentoring your children that must be addressed.

First, we communicate to our children, teenagers, and grandchildren through modeling. We must become before our kids and grandkids what, in our dreams, we want them to become. Our children, beginning at an early age, have a built-in "bunk detector." They recognize "bunk" when they hear or see it. When you say one thing and live another, everything you've said ends up in the "bunk" category.

I was teaching at a student leadership event once when a young man walked up to me and said, "Jerry you're dead wrong about this personal growth stuff." I asked, "What do you mean?" He continued, "All week long you've been saying that if we are going to grow to our maximum potential that we need to develop a personal growth plan, that is to read great books, listen to great tapes, surround ourselves with other winners, and sow seeds that benefit others. There is no way all of this is true. My dad comes home every day and watches television until bedtime. He either fishes or plays golf every weekend. I've never seen him do any of this stuff. If you were correct, my dad would be doing this!"

> *Children: Creatures who disgrace you by exhibiting in public the example that you set for them at home.*

What was happening? That young man was having to make up his mind between a few common sense, and I might add, widely accepted principles of personal growth, and what he saw reflected in his dad's everyday life. You cannot say to your kids, "No, you're not going to do this or that because you need to do your school work. Education is the key to life!" if you yourself have stopped growing personally. They will be thinking, "'If education is the key to life,' why aren't you still learning?" You can't say, "Why are you so self-centered? You only think of yourself," when you have a single mom next-door who struggles to take care of kids, get yard-work done, and hold down a full-time job, while you don't take time to pitch in and help. We must become before them what, in our dreams, we want them to become.

*The reason why anyone
refuses his assent to
your opinion,
or his aid to your
benevolent design,
is in you.
He refuses to accept you
as a bringer of truth,
because,
though you think you have it,
he feels that you have it not.
You have not given him
the authentic sign.*

—Ralph Waldo Emerson

Our behavior, not our words, reflects our true values. If we want to teach our children to think about others first, then we need to serve others as a family. If we believe integrity is a key value then we must only make promises that we know we can keep. Our kids must know they can take our word to the bank. Here is the point: The passion to be a winner is not taught–it's caught. What are we modeling? We have to be like the momma skunk and baby

> *Children seldom misquote you. In fact, they usually repeat word-for-word what you shouldn't have said.*

skunk going by the paper mill. The baby skunk stuck its tiny nostrils up in the air and filled them with that pungent paper mill odor and asked, "Momma, what on earth is that?" The momma skunk followed suit and said, "I don't know, but whatever it is we have got to have some of it." Our kids need to watch us and conclude that whatever we have, they want.

You might be thinking, "If modeling is that important, I've blown it." Don't fall for that self-talk, either. Don't believe it at all. We have all blown it at some point–there is no such thing as a perfect parent. My objective here is not to make you feel guilty about what you haven't done with your kids or your grandkids, but to challenge you to do the best with the rest of the time you have with them.

I have seen unbelievable things when a parent just walked up to a teenager and said, "I'm really sorry; I have not set a good example for you. Will you please forgive me? Let's start over." Teenagers are blown away by the vulnerability–start right now and do the best you can with the rest of the time that you have with them. Modeling is a must–the first and foremost way to communicate our values.

The second way we teach our children is through informal instruction. Informal instruction means that you teach as you walk along the normal traffic pattern of life. It doesn't mean that you sit down with an adolescent and say, "Pull out your pen and a notepad. I am going to give you a six point lecture on dealing with sexual pressure." Why? When you do that, the wall is up and you are finished before you start.

Consider for an example moral purity. How would you teach the importance of moral purity? I would encourage you to do a moral purity date. This can be an "as you go" kind of event. I used our monthly daddy-daughter date the first month of Paige's sixth grade year. We got seriously dressed up–when I get dressed up–it's a special event and I took her to a nice restaurant. Earlier that week, I had bought her a 14-karat gold promise ring. We talked about why she should wait for sex until she found that special young man. And even then, wait to have sex until after marriage. We not only discussed why to wait, but how to wait. I asked her to make a commitment to herself, to me, and to her future husband that he would be the first and the only, and it would be after they got married.

It was her choice and she made that commitment. Today she wears the ring as a reminder of that commitment. When she gets married, she plans to give it to her husband. I would challenge moms to take your sons and dads to take your daughters out on a similar event when they are between nine and eleven. Deal directly with these key questions and then keep the lines of communication open about them. If you would like information on discussing these issues, consult the *True Love Waits* website. The web information is included in the "Additional Suggested Resources" section at the end of this chapter.

If you struggle with your temper–flying off the handle, losing your cool, and saying things that you don't mean–please get a handle on that immediately. If you don't get a handle on it, two bad things are going to happen. First, there will be a time when your children and grandchildren will not respect you. We do not respect people who are consistently out of control. And second, when they need you the most you'll be among the last people they'll come to. They're not going to come to you when they've really messed up if they know you are a walking, breathing volcano waiting to erupt. If loss of control is an issue, I beg you to deal with it.

As you're taking your children to school, going to play golf together, going fishing, or whatever it is you like to do together, help them understand the world in which they live and to see it through the eyes of "informal instruction." This principle requires quality and quantity time together. I hear a lot of people say, "Well I don't spend a lot of time with my children but the time I do have with them is quality time." The only way you have quality time is if you have quantity time. As you are spending time together, help them understand the world they live in and life's enduring values through informal instruction.

The third way we mentor our children is through "family time." Here are a couple of ideas of what family time can be. **First, I would encourage you to find something inspirational to read together for a few minutes each day.** Many families use a mealtime for this. For my family, this is a night-time event. When you have it is not as important as the fact that you must have a consistent family time. I meet parents who use timeless literature or storybooks if they have small children. Those of you who come from a Christian frame of reference might want to use the Bible for this time of reflection. If you come from another faith perspective, you might want to use the appropriate holy book for that faith. Still other families might play a game. The important thing here is for the family to have a time everyday where they can talk about life's timeless values and reflect on the day.

Second, share concerns and needs with each other. Maybe the need or concern is related to a friend or loved one. Or it may be a concern at work or school. Parents, at least once a month share one of the areas you're struggling with and what you're doing to grow and develop in that area. Be sensitive and share from your heart. Share needs and struggles that are age-appropriate so that your children experience you as being real and vulnerable. Remember we're trying to teach them how to grow to their maximum potential–by example. If you're struggling with temper, for example, you could say, "I flew off the handle with mom earlier this evening; I have apologized to her and I want you to help hold me accountable to not say things I don't mean." Some parents think they can't be that vulnerable because their children would lose all respect for them. That's simply not true. In fact, children will respect you more for being honest, transparent, and for being vulnerable.

There was an old farmer nailing up a sign, "Puppies for sale." He had not even gotten the sign nailed up when this little guy walked over and said, "Mister, I want to buy one of your puppies." The farmer looked at the child and said, "Well son, these puppies are expensive. You probably can't even afford to look at one of these puppies. They cost a lot of money." The little fella dug into his overalls and asked, "Mister, would thirty-seven cents buy me a look?"

The old farmer realized what he had said and melted. He hollered at the mother dog, "Dolly, come here." Out of the barn came Dolly–a beautiful white dog followed by four little white fur balls, then the runt of the litter. The runt was a brown puppy–it literally rolled down the ramp and struggled to keep up with the others. The little fella said to the farmer, "Mister, I want that little brown puppy on the end."

The farmer answered and said, "You can't have that puppy. You can have any other one you want, but you can't have that one. That puppy is crippled and will never be able to run with you, jump with you, or keep up with you."

The little boy pulled up his overalls and exposed a brace on his leg and he said, "Mister, that's why I want that puppy–he is going to need somebody just like me who understands."

Neither your children nor your grandchildren will ever relate to perfection. They will never see perfection in us or experience it personally within themselves. What they can relate to is a mom, a dad, or maybe a grandparent who loves them unconditionally and is trying to grow to his or her maximum potential and is willing to talk about the struggle. So take the opportunity to share what is going on in your life.

Adding insulation adds value to any home by insuring the right atmosphere. Modeling, informal instruction, and a daily family time will provide the warm loving environment necessary to pass on life's timeless values to the next generation.

Put on Your Construction Hat and Let's Go to Work!

Consulting the Blueprint

What concepts from this chapter can I work on, learn, or practice?

These concepts will increase the value of my family in what ways?

What can I do to apply these principles in a practical way?

Building Blocks for My Home

With concepts from this chapter, what are practical steps I can take to build my family and create a "healthier" home?

One:

Two:

Three:

Basic Blocks For Building

I. There are many ways to share TIME–quality and quantity:
   -Model appropriate behavior to communicate values: social, emotional, physical, and spiritual.
   -Develop a Family Mission Statement.
   -Develop written Family Goals and Objectives.
   -Develop a Family Time:
      -Read books (library, novels, Bible, pop-up, etc).
      -Play games (Nertz, Rummikub, Scrabble, Yahtze, etc.).
      -Exercise together (walks, bikes, lift weights, etc.).
      -Eat meals at the table together.
      -Paint, color, draw, make things together.
      -Select and develop hobbies together.
      -Complete homework assignments with children and youth.
      -Internet surfing and exploration together.
      -Get to know your neighbors and serve others in the community.

II. Enhance the relationship with your child
   A. Do *With* Them:
      -Have meaningful conversation.   -Share unconditional love.
      -Do fun things that ***they*** like.   -Have Family Time.

B. Do *For* Them:
-Be stable and consistent.
-Provide a "safe questions" place.
-Provide safety/security.
-Work on yourself/marriage.

C. Do *Because of* Them:
-Work on yourself and marriage.
-Plan ahead and prepare.
-Enhance your family life.
-Spend quality/quantity time.

D. Do *In Spite of* Them:
-Be involved in their social life.
-Know their friends' families.
-Get involved in their school.
-Make rules and discipline.

III. Choose character qualities, personality traits, and characteristics that are important to you and your spouse for yourselves, your children, and your family. Some to consider (with opposites).

- Alertness vs. carelessness
- Attentiveness vs. distraction
- Availability vs. self-centeredness
- Benevolence vs. selfishness
- Boldness vs. fearfulness
- Caution vs. rashness
- Compassion vs. indifference
- Confidence vs. apprehension
- Consistence vs. unpredictable
- Contentment vs. covetousness
- Convictions vs. easily swayed
- Courage vs. fearful
- Creativity vs. underachievement
- Decisiveness vs. procrastination
- Dependability vs. unreliability
- Determination vs. fainthearted
- Diligence vs. slothfulness
- Discernment vs. shortsighted
- Discretion vs. simpleminded
- Doing Best vs. settling for less
- Endurance vs. discouragement

- Enthusiasm vs. apathy
- Fairness vs. self-serving
- Flexibility vs. rigidness
- Forgiveness vs. rejection
- Friendliness vs. arrogance
- Generosity vs. stinginess
- Gentleness vs. harshness
- Grateful vs. unthankfulness
- Honest vs. deceitfulness
- Honor vs. disrespect
- Hospitality vs. loneliness
- Humility vs. pride
- Initiative vs. idleness
- Joyfulness vs. self-pity
- Justice vs. corruption
- Kindness vs. rudeness
- Loving vs. selfish
- Loyalty vs. unfaithfulness
- Manners vs. unmannerly
- Meekness vs. anger
- Neatness vs. disorganized

- Obedience vs. willingness
- Orderliness vs. confusion
- Optimism vs. doubtful
- Patience vs. restlessness
- Persuasive vs. contentious
- Punctuality vs. tardiness
- Resourcefulness vs. wasteful
- Respectfulness vs. thankless
- Responsibility vs. unreliability
- Reverence vs. disregard
- Security vs. anxiety
- Self-Control vs. self-indulgence
- Sensitivity vs. callousness
- Servant vs. selfish
- Sincerity vs. hypocrisy
- Thankfulness vs. ungrateful
- Thoroughness vs. incomplete
- Thriftiness vs. extravagance
- Tolerance vs. prejudice
- Truthfulness vs. deception
- Unconditional Love vs.conditional
- Virtue vs. impurity
- Wisdom vs. foolishness
- Yield vs. doing it your own way

Additional Suggested Resources:

Campbell, Ross. *How to Really Love Your Children.*
Maxwell, John C. *Breakthrough Parenting.*
Pipes, Jerry and Victor Lee. *Family to Family.*
True Love Waits—contact them on line at: www.lifeway.com/tlw

Chapter VII.
Purchasing a Warranty—Building Internal Fences

When building a home, it is always wise to purchase a warranty. Even though you may have the best builder in the world, he is still depending on sub-contractors and they are depending on vendors to provide windows, doors, fixtures, wiring, appliances–you get the idea? A whole lot can go wrong with a house even with the best builder.

Children don't come with instructions or a warranty. I have written over and over on this principle but must say it again: Success is, first and foremost, success with self. It is an inside job. Discipline that comes closest to a home warranty is an inside job. I like to put it this way; discipline is building internal fences.

If discipline does not remain an inside job, then you and I have failed as parents. Remember, success is knowing your purpose in life, growing to your maximum potential, and sowing seeds that benefit others. So, in everything we do with discipline, we are trying to help our children and grandchildren learn to

> ### *A healthy parent is what makes a healthy kid!*

make choices themselves that result in them becoming the best they can be because that's what they want to do. Remember you always begin with the end in mind. As you think about discipline, think where you're trying to go ultimately. Not just in the short-term, but in the long run–where do you want to end up? Then, begin with that end in mind.

Three basic parenting styles

There are three basic parenting styles. If you were to read books on parenting you would consistently read about these. Although some authors use different terms, the ideas would essentially be the same. I am going to share them with you in order of the most common to the least.

The first and most common one would be permissive parenting. Most parents are permissive parents. A permissive parent is a parent who loves their child, loves their grandchild, and wants the best for them. But in my opinion they really don't know how to love them. Here's the problem; they want so much to be their child's friend that they're not willing to do what's best for them. We have a huge, huge number of co-dependent people who are parents. These moms and dads are looking to gain their own sense of self-worth and self-esteem from their children. You have a serious problem if you need the love and acceptance of your child or your grandchild to make you feel good about yourself. Why? If you need them and their approval, you cannot lead them. If you are dependent upon them to meet your needs, you can't provide what is best for them. You are constantly caught between doing what is best for them and your need to have them like you. Two co-dependent people in an interdependent situation is like having two ticks and no dog. You must first be independent before you can be interdependent. A permissive parent, generally, is one who loves the children but does not really know how to love them.

The second parenting style is authoritarian parenting. An authoritarian parent loves their children and grandchildren, but they're so hard and firm that it's difficult for the child to see and experience their love. Every deliberation tends to begin and end with, "It's going be this way because I said so." Remember, they love their kids; it's just hard for children to realize the love when every discussion begins and ends with, "There will be no discussion."

> *How can a stranger tell*
> *if two people are married?*
> *You might have to guess based*
> *on whether they seem to be*
> *yelling at the same kids.*
> *—Derrick, age 8*

The third most used parenting style is authoritative parenting. This used to be called democratic parenting, but there is really nothing about this parenting style that resembles a democracy. It's not like having a discussion. Everybody gets a vote and the majority rules. Mom and dad try hard and always give kids the right to feel what they feel, to share what they want to share, and to get a vote in the family. However, an authoritative parent always reserves the right to hold the trump card. They always reserve the right to say, "While I understand why you do not want to go to this event, when the bus leaves you are going to be on the bus." Another example would be, "I understand that you want to date John and why; however, here is the reason that I will not allow you to do so." With this style of parenting, mom and dad always reserve the right to hold the trump card. This is especially tough when the child is strong-willed.

You might be having a hard time with allowing your kids to express their objections. Remember, the key to a long-term warranty is internal fence building. If your kids aren't involved in the decision-making process until they leave your home, you might not be pleased with the long-term results.

Tommy was standing up in class when the teacher said, "Tommy, I want you to sit down." Tommy answered, "No!" and continued to stand. "Tommy, I want you to sit down now." Tommy said, "No!" and continued standing. Finally, the teacher said, "Tommy, I want you to sit down right now or I'm going to rip your ears off" (slight exaggeration). Tommy finally sat down but turned to his friend next to him and said, "On the inside, I'm still standing up!" You can bet he stood up again at his first opportunity.

You can, for the most part, make your kids do what you want them to do while they live in your house. But when they leave your house, they're going do what they want to do. So, the key is, how do we parent so that when they leave our house at age eighteen, they choose to be winners? Some people have a real hard time with the fact that authoritative parenting means our kids have the freedom to question us.

I want to encourage you that while it is at times easier to be authoritarian in our parenting, the authoritarian style does not work over the long term as our kids move into the adolescent years. In fact, it most often backfires.

What is the best way to parent? In my opinion here is a good timeline to follow. The best parenting style from birth through kindergarten would be a loving, caring, unconditionally-accepting authoritarian parent. Young children need two basic things: They need unconditional love and acceptance and they need to learn to respond to authority. If you allow a two year old to demand to know "Why," you are making a serious mistake. "Because I said so" is fine for a two year old. If they don't learn to respond to your authority as a preschooler, then they will struggle with all authority structures and figures and ultimately have to be broken in adolescence. America's prisons are full of those who were never disciplined as a teenager.

One afternoon Debra and I walked out of a conference in Mississippi, put Paige and Josh in their car seats, got in the van, and this lady said, "How did you do that?" I said, "How did we do what?" She said, "There's nothing I can do to make my three year old stay in his car seat." How sad. Here was a thirty-five year old mother who had surrendered the reigns of control and authority in her home to her three year old child.

We fought the battle over the car seat when Paige was about two years old. It was very embarrassing. A friend picked us up at the airport and Paige began crying for Debra to hold her as we left the parking lot. There was nothing physically wrong with her; she had just decided on a public forum to test the boundaries on the car seat issue. After about five minutes we finally told her, "No matter how much you cry, you're staying in this car seat."

> ## The best discipline in the world is reality discipline.

From the airport in Little Rock, Arkansas until within ten miles of our destination–almost two hours, Paige cried. She did not want to be in that car seat. But, she stayed there and that was the last time she ever cried about being in the car seat. She learned that it didn't matter if she turned red, purple, green, or yellow; she was not getting out of the car seat. That battle was over!

She was dry, she was fed, there was nothing wrong except for the fact she was mad about being in the car seat. She didn't need a spanking; she needed reality. We never went through that battle with Josh. Why? Paige took care of it. One day Josh started complaining about being in the car seat; Paige told him not to waste his time crying about it. It wouldn't work.

Here is the point: Preschoolers through kindergartners cannot be in charge of our homes. They need unconditional love and acceptance, and they need to learn to respond to authority.

The second age group is children from about the first grade through about the fifth grade. The line of authority should go up ever so slightly. You are basically an authoritarian parent, but you begin to let the children make some decisions on their own with direction. For example, you would walk in with three outfits and ask, "Christie, which one of these outfits would you like to wear today?" She is beginning to make the choices, but you're deciding what the parameters of the choices are.

By the time a child hits middle school, you need to be a full-blown authoritative parent. Everything is up for discussion. If they don't want to go to school, let's talk with them about it. If they don't want to go to practice, let's talk with them about it. If they want to start staying up later, let's talk with them about it. Everything is up for discussion. But you always reserve the right at the end of the conversation to say, "While I understand how you feel, this is where the boundaries are going to be and why." Authoritative parents give their teenagers more and more freedom as they earn the right to have it. How do they earn it? Through responsible and trustworthy behavior.

Hints for effective internal fence building

First, as a parent, you must decide on your goals for discipline. Begin with the end in mind. Ultimately, what are you trying to accomplish? For Debra and me, our goal for discipline with our children is to teach them to be self-disciplined. In other words, our goal is for them to leave our home having decided for themselves to be the best they can be. Everything we do in discipline boils right back down to that statement. We want them to be winners who discover their purpose in life, grow to their maximum potential, and sow seeds that benefit others.

Each parent must decide what their ultimate goal is for discipline. Remember that a successful family is built around core values. The difference between animals and people is that people have the right and freedom to choose. Animals are born with, and are driven by, instinct. But, people have the ability to choose, and the ability to choose assumes values.

Second, embrace their drive for independence. It is normal and necessary for them to desire independence. While it's painful to you as a parent, believe me, you want a pulling away to occur. You do not want them at thirty years old with their spouse and kids in your home permanently. You want them to be independent. I know a man who said, "I really struggled with this whole empty nest syndrome." He said he struggled with it for about seven or eight minutes and from then on, it's been great. Accept their drive for independence as normal and necessary.

Third, realize they want you to be tough. Some of you are thinking, "This guy has just lost his mind." No, they want you to be tough. It's true. It is also a fact that every child will test and break your rules or limits no matter where you place them. I don't care how permissive you are or how firm. It doesn't matter how tight or how far out the boundaries are. They will test and break them. Believe it or not, deep down in their hearts, they want you to be tough. They know when you are firm it means you love them.

My dad had been a Sergeant in the Marines. He would walk into my room some mornings while I was sound asleep, "Hup, two, three, four. Hup, two, three, four." He was still a full-blooded Marine at heart.

I had a friend growing up who was great to spend the night with. His mom and dad both drank a lot. By 11:00 p.m., they were usually out for the night. We finished off what was left in the alcohol department and then went out running around until two or three o'clock in the morning. I loved spending the night with him. However, he was almost always at our house; recently, we watched all the "Pipes family" movies, and he was in everything. He was on most vacations and at almost every major family event. He grew up at our house. Now why would somebody raised by loose standards choose to live in a house with a Marine when he could stay home and have few rules?

Recently, at my father's funeral, this friend explained it this way, "Jerry, your dad was as tough as a boot but we always knew he loved us and wanted the best for us."

I promise you this: Your kids are going to push and scream. They will tell you how unfair you are and how everybody else gets to do everything you are saying no to. But deep down in their hearts, they want you to be tough because they know that when you are strict and have rules, it means that you care.

> ## Kids learn through reality:
>
> **When your mom is mad at your dad, don't let her brush your hair.**
>
> **If your sister hits you, don't hit her back. They always catch the second person.**
>
> **Never hold a dust-buster and a cat at the same time.**

Fourth, set up rules that allow you to be as positive as possible. Remember, you'll be saying "no" an awful lot. So pick your battles. There are some things that really are not worth wasting the emotional energy over. If your teenagers are struggling with major issues, it would probably be smart to not make a big deal out of whether or not their room is like you want it to be. Remember, authoritative parents extend the boundaries allowing more and more freedom as their teenagers earn the right to have it. Having rules that allow you to be positive means that you start with tight boundaries so you can reward responsible behavior with more freedom. If you give up too much territory up front, you have less to work with.

Fifth, teach your children through reality discipline. All children, regardless of age, must experience the consequences of their behavior. Notice that I am saying, "Teach through reality discipline." Discipline is about instruction–remember, we are internal fence building (self-discipline). Reality discipline is the only discipline that will get you to self-discipline. I'm not saying you shouldn't spank your child during the early years, especially for defiant behavior. However, by the time they get to be older elementary age or middle school age, you need to be building internal fences through reality discipline.

Principles For Spanking:

Never spank while you are angry–you need to be in control of your emotions.

Spanking should be rare–reserve it for disrespectful, defiant behavior.

Follow this sequence: Affirmation, clearly explain the reason for the spanking, spank, and follow up with love and acceptance.

So, what is reality discipline? It is developing boundaries, establishing natural consequences, and being consistent in enforcement. This is the only discipline that truly works. We all, young and old, learn through reality.

Let me give you some examples all the way through from bed babies to teenagers. Think about the idea of putting a young child to bed and having them sleep all night. We know that by several months of age, children are old enough to be sleeping all night. Doctors say that it is healthy for children and healthy for parents when they sleep all night.

> *Excellence is not an act, but a habit. —Aristotle*

When my daughter was seven months old, at the doctor's advice, we stopped feeding her in the middle of the night. She was dry, fed, and finally healthy (thank God for tubes!). We put her in bed, kissed her and assured her of our love, turned off the light and of course, she began to do some serious crying, turning first red, then blue, and finally purple. Okay, slight exaggeration, but she did not want to be in bed.

On several occasions, I literally thought I might have to tie Debra to the bed to keep her from going in to pick up Paige. On that first night we tried the reality discipline approach, it took 18 minutes and 37 seconds of unbelievable, heart wrenching crying. We wondered if we were being terrible parents to this child, but we did not go into her room. Had we gone in, she would have said, "Gotcha." But after 18 minutes and 37 seconds, she realized no one was coming to her rescue, so she went to sleep. At about two in the morning, she was ready for her two o'clock feeding. Our doctor told us, "Don't give her formula; give her water instead." This turn of events really made Paige mad; she had always been fed at two o'clock in the morning. My wife took her a bottle of water which led to several minutes of crying after which she slept the rest of the night.

The next night it didn't take 18 minutes and 37 seconds, it took about eleven minutes of crying. She realized the night before, no one showed up in eighteen minutes so she gave up at eleven minutes. She didn't even get up at two in the morning–why? Why get up for water?

The third night it took about six minutes and the fourth night about three and you know what? We were done.

It wasn't a fun week, but we were done. I have related this story all over the world. It is very rare that I don't have at least one parent walk up after and say something like this, "I wish I had done that; my son is five and he still sleeps with us." Kids learn through reality!

> ## *Kids learn through reality!*

Anytime you have a strong-willed child or a very intelligent one, there are going to be major battles along the way that you absolutely–100 percent, MUST not lose. If you lose, you will pay for it for a long, long time. I'll never forget the time that my daughter decided to really test us. She was twenty-three months old and we were in the process of preparing to leave for a five-week business trip in California. The entire family was going.

We took a break from packing to put my daughter to bed. We had a rule in our house at that time that once we put Paige to bed she could not get out of bed without permission, or the consequences would be a spanking. No questions. As you well know, adults with small children have to fight to keep some privacy. My wife and I were packing, getting ready to go on a five-week trip and my daughter got out of bed less than a minute after we turned off the light. We still have her beautiful flannel

PJ's to remember this event. My daughter stood there with her arms crossed defiantly and she said, "Mommy and Daddy, I'm not going to go to sleep until you go to sleep. And when I do go to sleep, I'm going to sleep with you."

It took everything we could do just to keep from dying laughing; she was just so cute! But I picked her up in her little PJ's and I had a choice to make: Laugh or take a stand.

Here is a key principle with reality discipline: Don't draw the lines if you don't plan to do what you promised when they cross them.

Reality discipline does not work when children get second, third, fourth chances, and unlimited tries. When a child crosses the line, whatever consequence you set must happen the first time. As much as I did not want to, I took her to her bedroom, affirmed her, explained that she was getting a spanking because that is what we promised would happen if she crossed this particular line. I gave her the spanking, told her how much I loved her, and put her back in bed. I thought that would be the end of it, but I was barely back in the living room when Paige made her re-entrance less than thirty seconds later.

To make a long story much shorter, an hour and twenty minutes and multiple spankings later, she finally decided the boundary we had set was real and she was going to stay in her bed. Reality discipline means you draw the lines and when children cross them, whatever consequences you promised happens on the first violation.

That is the only major confrontation we've ever had with my daughter thus far. She learned, on that cold February evening, that when we draw the line–the boundary is really there. I've learned that kids love to take social situations and use them on mom and dad.

Another area of setting limits is with the issue of mealtime and eating habits, especially when company is present. Several years ago, we had close friends with two boys. We enjoyed spending time with this family and ate at their house often–but it finally became too frustrating to be there and watch the interaction between the father and his boys at meal times. The boys were five and seven–sharing a meal with them was like eating with animals. They would throw food, run around, and all kinds of things. It wasn't fun.

This couple would invite us over to eat often and reminded us of how much they enjoyed having us in their home. After we stopped going, they continually invited us and we simply made excuses. Finally, one day the father asked, "Why won't you come over and eat with us anymore?" And I said, "Do you really want to know? I don't want to offend you, but if you really want to know, I'll tell you." He wanted to know, so I said, "To be honest with you, I cannot watch you relate to your boys; you threaten them and you threaten them and you don't ever do what you tell them you're going to do. That's why they don't respect nor obey you."

He confessed to being frustrated as well, and asked, "What do you think I ought to do?" I responded in love, "Do you honestly want to know what I think? Because if you don't want to know what I think, I probably shouldn't answer. If you want to know what I think, I'll be happy to discuss it with you." He was eager for a solution so I shared my thoughts, "Here's what I think you ought to do. You ought to say to your boys, 'If you don't want to eat, you don't have to eat. If you'd rather play, you can play. When it comes to mealtime, if you want to eat you can eat, but if you don't, there's going to be nothing until breakfast in the morning. There will not be cookies or milk; you can't have orange juice, or apple juice. Your stomach is going to feel like your throat has been cut, but you can have nothing until tomorrow.'"

I continued to the father, "If you're not going to follow through, don't draw these lines."

He did it! He sat the boys down and did just as I had suggested. I was impressed. His boys were slow learners, they went to bed hungry three times. They finally realized if they didn't sit down and eat they weren't going to get

> **We all, regardless of age, learn through reality.**

another shot. We ate with them several months after that and it was fun; the boys were different human beings.

I had a speaking engagement in Texas once and this dad walked up and said to me, "Jerry, what do I do with my son? I'm the most unpopular man in my community right now because of my son." Here is the story: His son had just turned sixteen years old. On his sixteenth birthday, this man bought a brand new sports car and gave it to him. Now, I personally think that sends a wrong message to a child–in life, things are not free. To his credit, the car was given with some seriously tight boundaries. He said, "If you break the law and get a ticket, you are not going anywhere on weekends for a month and you are grounded from this car for two months."

His son got a ticket on the way home from a football game. The ticket was for speeding; the son was going 80 miles per hour in a 55 speed zone.

The next week happened to be Homecoming. The mother of his girlfriend had purchased a $200 dress, on sale, and couldn't get her money back. This father was getting calls from all kinds of people in the community, "What is your problem? Why don't you defer punishment for one week? Why is this girl going to pay the price because of your son's mistake? Why does her mom have to pay? She can't get her money back on this dress."

He came to me and asked, "Jerry, what do I do? Am I being too hard?" Here was my suggestion: "Your son knew the speed limit was 55, he chose to drive 80. He knew if he got a ticket he was grounded for a month, and from the car for two months. I think if you didn't intend to hold his feet to the fire you should not have drawn the lines to start with."

You won't believe what this guy did; not only did his son not go to Homecoming, but for the very first time in his son's entire life, he had to get a job to pay his girlfriend's mother back for the $200 dress.

I could give you example after example after example. Draw the lines and when children cross them, whatever you promised in terms of consequences must happen the first time. For me, the hardest part of being a parent is not knowing what to do, rather doing what's right in this area when I am emotionally and physically exhausted. Being consistent with reality discipline is hard work. It sounds easy and it's effective, but it will demand great sacrifice. If you're reading this as a mom, this is a lot harder for you than it is for dads. Why? You're around the kids more, and they wear you down. But, the way to keep them from wearing you down is to be consistent. It's harder up front, but it pays in the long haul.

Please, note, that the above consequences were natural consequences. Also, if both parents are at home it is important to agree on a course of action and be consistent. Dealing with one parent must be the same as relating to the other. Otherwise, your kids will drive a wedge between you.

By the way, if you have a middle-schooler or a teenager, every rule deserves a reason. If they say, "Why?" You need to answer that question. Our goal is to help them learn how to make positive life choices. However, there comes a point at which you've had the discussion fifteen times and you can and should say, "We've already discussed that, you understand why we have this rule, this discussion is over." When the issue becomes a threat to your authority, you need to deal with it in that light. Remember, they need to know why because we're trying to help them make life choices.

One final principle: get involved in your child's social life. Neither your child nor your teenager should ever, ever, ever spend the night at someone's house if you don't know that family. You need to get involved in their social life. They shouldn't attend an event you have not checked out. Children will often say something like, "Mom, Tim's parents are letting him go to the party; can I go?" What you

> ### *Get involved in their social life.*

don't know is that Tim is telling his parents that you're letting your kid go; can he go? The kids talk among themselves–and work these things out and parents don't generally talk to corroborate stories.

They should never, ever, ever attend a party that you have not checked out thoroughly. Parents who get offended by our questions generally have a reason to be offended. You wouldn't believe how many parents reason like this: "They're going to drink anyway so we're going to provide it and let them stay here. At least they're not going to drink and drive."

Not being involved in your teenager's life and not asking questions will produce tremendous pain for all involved. I was speaking in Los Angeles one time and was walking across the lobby of a hotel. The young teenager in front of me was on her cell phone saying, "Mom, this is Crissy, I'm leaving Jennifer's house and will be home in twenty minutes."

This fourteen year old spent the night in a hotel with her boyfriend because mom and dad didn't get involved in her social life.

One day I was doing an assembly in an Oklahoma school and a young lady walked up to me and said, "My boyfriend raped me last night; was it my fault?" I said, "Your boyfriend raped you? What in the world are you talking about?" She said, "Well, I told my mom and dad that I was going to be going camping with a girlfriend and her family." Mom and dad never called. She went camping with her girlfriend and their boyfriends. The guys were drinking, they started fondling, and when she asked her boyfriend to get off, he didn't. "My boyfriend raped me; is it my fault?" In reality, the blame lies with her, her boyfriend, and both sets of parents.

As parents, we must get involved in their social life which means getting to know the people involved in our children's lives, their families, and helping our children make responsible choices about friends. Our kids' close friends have a huge impact on them.

Remember, the best warranty with our children is internal fences. If we can help our kids: Develop a worthwhile dream that drives them, core values that guide them, a personal growth plan that develops them, experience consequences that shape them, and choose friends that help them be their best, then we will have moved a long way down the road on internal fence building.

Put on Your Construction Hat and Let's Go to Work!

Consulting the Blueprint

What concepts from this chapter can I work on, learn, or practice?

These concepts will increase the value of my family in what ways?

What can I do to apply these principles in a practical way?

Building Blocks for My Home

With concepts from this chapter, what are practical steps I can take to build my family and create a "healthier" home?

One:

Two:

Three:

Basic Blocks For Building

-Allow children to experience consequences of their own decisions.
-Be as positive as possible.
-Provide clear understanding of rewards and punishments.
-Provide a list of consequences for poor and unacceptable behavior.
-Provide a chore chart for them to understand and see responsibilities.
-Get involved in their social life: Allow them to have friends in your home, invite their friends to spend time with your family, and know their friends, their friend's families, and destinations.

Chore Chart   for _____ (name)
week of _____ to _____

Chore	Mon	Tue	Wed	Thu	Fri	Sat	Sun
Brush Teeth							
Brush Hair							
Make Bed							
Clean Room							
Laundry							
Dishes							
Sweep							
Mop							
Trash							
Others:							

Unacceptable Behavior and Discipline Chart
Having your bedroom "unreasonably" dirty:
   1st time it happens:_____
   2nd time it happens:_____

Making or leaving a mess in common areas of home:
   1st time it happens:_____
   2nd time it happens:_____

Having to be asked to do something two or more times:
   1st time it happens:_____
   2nd time it happens:_____

Being home late after going somewhere:
   1st time it happens:_____
   2nd time it happens:_____

Not letting an adult/assigned babysitter know where you are:
   1st time it happens:_____
   2nd time it happens:_____

Intentionally doing something that you are not supposed to do:
   1st time it happens:_____
   2nd time it happens:_____

Being rude or inappropriately disrespectful to a member of family:
   1st time it happens:_____
   2nd time it happens:_____
Each additional time it happens: Consequences will be arranged on an as-needed basis with mom/dad/adult.

Additional Suggested Resources:
Dobson, James. *Bringing up Boys.*
Dobson, James. *The New Dare to Discipline.*
Leman, Kevin. *Making Children Mind Without Losing Yours.*
Leman, Kevin. *Smart Kids Stupid Choices.*

Section Four

Rebuilding From Storms, Neglect, or Other Disasters

> **Every dewdrop of rain had a whole lot of heaven with it.**
> **—Henry Wadsworth Longfellow**

Chapter VIII.
Protecting Your Home—Moving Through the Tough Times

Prepare today for the storms of tomorrow

There were two elementary girls in Florida who were brutally and repeatedly raped by family members. Many years afterward, one of them said, "How can you expect me to be anything other than an alcoholic? I was raped as a little girl." The other one said, "At age twenty-one, I'm going to prove even though I was molested that I can make something of my life," and she became the first female Senator from the State of Florida. How do the tough times impact you? Do they make you bitter or better?

I have noticed several trends as I relate to people and observe how the tough times impact them. There are some people who deal with tough times through the escape method. They try to escape through a pill, a bottle, a relationship, or any number of other things. They try to eat away the difficulties. The problem with the escape method is that it just multiplies the problems. If you have a problem and you abuse alcohol to escape from it, then, you wake-up with your original problem times a hang over. If you try to eat away the difficulty, then, you wake-up with your original problem times health problems and lower self-worth and self-esteem. The escape method just multiplies the difficulties.

Then there is the denial method. People who utilize the denial method stick their heads in the sand and say, "This is not happening to me; this is not happening." The prob-

> ## *Denying reality won't lessen the impact!*

lem with the denial method is that denying the reality of the difficulties won't change the impact they have on your life. Imagine that you are hit by a dump truck–POW! Do you simply say to yourself, "This is not happening to me? My nose is not in my shirt pocket. My arm is not across the street. Further, they are not sweeping me into this bag." Denying the reality of difficulties won't change the impact they have on your life.

There is also the positive thinking method. These people read self-help books and check out PMA tapes (Positive Mental Attitude). They think if they can grin and bear it for long enough, they will be able to gut it out and move on beyond the tough times.

Finally, there is the cop-out method. These are the people who commit suicide. Just recently I heard about a man who lost his job and was struggling financially; out on the back deck of his house, he put a pistol in his mouth, pulled the trigger, and left his young wife with three small children to pick up the pieces of their lives.

Suicide is the most selfish, self-centered, cop-out on life that I know anything about. Not only that, but 99% of the problems we face in this life are temporary. Suicide is a permanent solution to a temporary problem. It's not a very smart way to handle the difficulties.

How do you handle the tough times? By the way, if you haven't already figured this out, you are going to have tough times–individually and in the family. It's not "if" you have them–but when you have them. When the tough times come, how will you deal with them?

Every week I hear so many things:
- ◆ My husband of thirty years is having an affair.
- ◆ My teenager was just killed in a car accident.
- ◆ Mom and dad are getting a divorce.
- ◆ We just filed bankruptcy.
- ◆ My child just died.

Three principles in dealing with the tough times

Prepare today for the storms of tomorrow. Over the years I have watched people deal with amazing doses of pain with incredible grace. They display a sense of peace, a sense of wellness and even though their world is falling down about them, there is a sense of peace that comes from deep down inside. The best picture of this that I've ever seen was back in the mid-eighties. A thirty-seven year old woman shared this story. Her husband of eleven years stopped to be a good Samaritan to a hitchhiker. The hitchhiker got into her husband's car and stabbed him sixty-seven times from the waist up, then, threw his body into the trunk of his own car. Her husband was obviously very, very dead. Next, the hitchhiker drove 500 miles to the border of Texas and Mexico, threw the body into a ditch, and according to the coroner, drove the man's own car back and forth over the body forty-five to fifty times. The man's body was totally mutilated.

What do you say to a thirty-seven year old lady whose husband has been brutalized like that? I didn't know what to say to her, but I didn't need to know. She took me by the hand and said, "Jerry, isn't God good? He gave us eleven unbe-lievable years of marriage and I know somehow he's going to make something

> ## *Look for the silver lining!*

good out of what I don't understand." She wasn't happy about what hap-pened to her husband, but she was able to face it with a sense of peace, a sense of wellness, that God would somehow bring something good out of her pain.

Think about the word "trials." This is an unbelievable word. In com-mon Greek, the root word for the word "trials" is the same root word that is used to describe an ambush. If you could get prepared to be ambushed, you'd never be ambushed. In an ambush, you're walking down the street, minding your own business, and somebody jumps from behind a dumpster or a building, and they attack you suddenly and unexpectedly.

Here is the point, you cannot prepare for the tough times. The lady that I described to you was from Houston, Texas. She didn't hear that her husband was missing on Friday, run down to her church, and take a crash course on how to deal with tough times. That's not why she was so strong. She was strong, because eleven years earlier, she had discovered faith in Christ. For eleven years she had been growing strong in her walk with God. And because she was strong in her faith she was ready to face her tough time when it came.

You prepare for the tough times of tomorrow–if they come next week, next month, next year–by growing strong today: By discovering your individual purpose in life and as a family, developing core values, growing to your maximum potential, and sowing seeds that benefit others.

Do your priorities reflect that your life is being well spent? Are you organizing and prioritizing your life around your established purpose for life and core values? You can answer these questions by evaluating three things:

- ◆ Where do you spend your time? If you want to know what your priorities are, just look at your calendar.
- ◆ Where do you spend your money? Look at your checkbook.
- ◆ What do you dream about? Even more important than the first two, believe it or not, is when you daydream–when you're driving down the highway listening to the radio of your own imagination–what are you daydreaming about?

Learning Through the Storms

When we go through difficult times, it is easy to get depressed if we spend our time focusing on the mess rather than what we can learn through it. When things are really going south with your kids or your spouse or at work, ask, "What can I learn through these difficulties?" It always helps to think about something you can control or think positively about.

> *Dear GOD: Thank you for the baby brother, but what I prayed for was a puppy. —Joyce, age 5*

Why do seemingly bad things happen to good people? Why do seemingly bad things happen to good families? I have found in relating to my pain and in working with parents and students for almost thirty years, that most difficulties fall into three categories.

First, there is the issue of testing. I'm told that potato farmers in Idaho never sort out their potatoes before they go to market. They put them in the back of these big trucks, drive over the roughest roads in the county and as the trucks bounce along, the big potatoes end up at the top, the medium size potatoes in the middle, and the little micro cosmic potatoes at the bottom. That's what tough times do for us. They help us know where we are.

There was a boy named Johnny. He walked up to his friend Jimmy and said, "My dad has a list of men in our town that he can whip, and your dad is at the top of the list." Well, that really angered Jimmy because his dad played in the National Football League. He was about 6'5" or 6'6"–he was huge. He could still bench press about five or six-hundred pounds. He was very proud of the fact that his dad could beat up anybody. Well, Jimmy was upset so he went home and told his dad. His dad got mad and went over to Johnny's house to confront Johnny's father. Johnny's dad answered the door and Jimmy's dad said, "I hear that you have a list of all the men in this city you can whip, and I'm at the top of the list." Johnny's dad said, "That's right." The former NFL star said, "You can't do it" as he steps up to the same level with Johnny's dad. At this point, he is looking down at him. Johnny's dad looks up, sees the huge chest, sees the bulging biceps, and said, "You know, I think I'll just take your name off the list."

> *The ultimate measure of a man is not where he stands in moments of comfort and convenience, but where he stands at times of challenge and controversy.*
>
> —*Martin Luther King, Jr.*

We never know where we really stand until we're tested. Testing is one of the character-building principles of life. Testing is good for us. It may be that your tough time will reveal a character flaw, or help you overcome an area of weakness. It might build your character.

Second, it could be that your difficulties will be used to help you add value to others.
I'll never forget a little thirteen year old girl that my wife and I met a number of years ago. I found out a few weeks after we met her that her dad had been molesting her every week for five years. We worked with the District Attorney and got him put in prison. I have often thought about that little girl. She had been so broken but over time, she developed a dream worth living for, established core values, grew to her maximum potential, and today serves others. For several years, she worked in one of our large cities helping prostitutes come out of that destructive lifestyle. As she started sharing with prostitutes about healing and what they could become, they would look at her and say, "Listen, if you had been through what I have been through, you wouldn't be talking to me about my choices in life. Life isn't fair." When those prostitutes said that to her, she had quite a story to tell.

She helped a lot of hurting ladies take responsibility for their choices. She helped ladies take back their lives, begin to make their own decisions, which changed the direction of their lives for good. They saw "hope" in her life. Was she excited that her dad's destructive choices hurt her deeply? No. But, she didn't let his poor decisions mess up her life. She took life's lemons and made lemonade.

Third, the difficulties of life often serve as a source of correction.
I think if we are honest, we all would have to admit that there have been times when our pain has been self-inflicted. When I am going through the fire, I always ask myself, "Have I done anything that created or contributed to this mess?" Over the years there have been occasions when these questions revealed my tough times were brought on by my poor choices. This recognition and the decision to make a course correction made the difficulty worthwhile. My football coach used to say that, "Dumb is when you do the same things over and over and expect different results." Often if we kicked the person most responsible for our difficulties, none of us could sit down for a week.

Wait patiently and hang onto your values through the tough times.
A young man named Brian from Provo, Utah had what we might all agree to be the worst day in history. Now imagine this day. He was awakened one morning by leaking plumbing. The water was ankle-deep

in his room. He decided to call his landlord. But he had a phone with an answering machine that was plugged into the wall. He thought, "If I'm standing in water and get on the phone, I'll be shocked."

He sat down on his bed and called his landlord. The landlord said, "What you need to do is go down and get a water vac, then clean up the water. I'll send a plumber, and everything will be fine." So Brian went out of his room, down to his car and found that he not only had a room full of water, but also had a flat tire on his car. So, he fixed the flat and thought to himself, "I don't have enough time to get the water vac, clean up the room, and make my meeting, so I'll call for help."

He ran upstairs and got back on the phone, forgetting he was standing ankle-deep in water (remember the phone is plugged into the wall) and he was shocked big-time. As he jumped back, he ripped the phone out of the wall and now he couldn't call for help. He ran back downstairs only to discover his car, which he had left running, had been stolen.

There is a silver lining in the story because the car didn't have a lot of gas, so he didn't think the car thief would get far. With the help of a friend, he was able to find and retrieve his car, get some gas, get the water vac, clean up some of the water, and get dressed for his meeting. He ran downstairs again and jumped into the driver's seat–forgetting that he had left his bayonet lying in the driver's seat. You guessed it! He sat on the bayonet. A bayonet is a long knife–it's very sharp. It was made to attach to the end of a rifle. It made a very definite "impression" on the right side of his back side. Now instead of going to his meeting, he had to go to the hospital because of the cut on his backside. He went into the hospital where they did some strategic surgery on the bayonet wound. He was groggy because of the anesthetic. He went back into his room, forgetting how wet the floor was, and slipped and fell injuring his lower back. He couldn't move. He had to lie there for two hours. When the meeting was finally over, someone came to check on him–found him lying on the floor, and took him to the hospital because of the back injury. By the time he got there, reporters in the city had heard about his day and showed up for the story.

They asked him, "Brian, how do you figure this kind of a day?" He answered, "Well, I think God was trying to kill me, but He just kept on missing."

Now, I shared that long story with you, which, by the way, is a true story–to simply ask if there has ever been a time in your life–and please be honest with yourself, that things were so bad that you thought, "There is no way that I can abide by my values and have what I want to have, or be what I want to be?" Have you ever felt like that before? "There has to be another way, because my values are not going to work." "I can't stay married to this person anymore and be happy." "I am tired of sacrificing for these kids." "What about what I want out of life?" "Why should I put up with this emotional abuse?"

Sound familiar? If you are like most people, you have felt all these things and more. I have been there, and done that. It is normal!

While it's normal at times to want to give up, the difference between success and failure is remembering your dreams, hanging onto your core values, and paying the price for an awesome family.

> ***I do the very best I know how–the very best I can–and mean to keep doing so until the end.***
> ***—Abraham Lincoln***

There is a man who is a lot like me, in that he travels a lot. Every time he goes somewhere, he brings a surprise for his two boys. He was on his way home from the airport and he realized, "I forgot gifts for the boys." He knows that the guys are going to peck him on the cheek and go for the suitcase. So, he quickly scrambles and decides what he is going to do. He gets home and the boys peck him on the cheek, they're digging in the suitcase and he said, "Boys, you're wasting your time; there's nothing there for you. But, tomorrow you get the best surprise ever. Tomorrow, instead of going to school, we're going to the mall. When the mall opens at ten o'clock, we're going inside and I want you to listen up boys, here are the ground rules: You can have anything you want, anything."

The next day, the boys were so excited. They got to the mall and to a big candy counter in the mall and said, "Dad, can we have a bag full of these Reese's Pieces?" He said, "Boys, you can have a bag full of

Reese's Pieces if you want, but listen to me: You can have anything you want. You might want to look a little further–there might be something just a little bit better than Reese's Pieces."

They started looking around and went into a toy store and found some Power Ranger suits. They said, "Dad, we've always wanted Power Ranger suits, can we have them?" He said, "I will buy you whatever you want, but you might want to look a little further than Power Ranger suits because there might be something even better than that." They went into the sporting goods section and found these Michael Jordan, NBA leather basketballs. They were about $100 each. They said, "Dad, can we have these leather basketballs?" They thought they were pushing the envelope.

Dad said, "Listen, I brought you here to buy you anything you want, but you might even find something better than basketballs if you just keep looking." They ended up at the back of the store and found these brand-new bikes; they were the weird colors and were about $400 a pop. They said, "Dad, could we have these bikes?" The dad lit up and said, "I brought you to the mall today to buy you these bikes."

Way too often, in the midst of the difficult times, we forget our purpose in life, ignore our values, stop growing, and allow ourselves to become bitter. Sometimes, in the process of life, we sacrifice what is best for our families and settle for life's Reese's Pieces.

Put on Your Construction Hat and Let's Go to Work!

Consulting the Blueprint

What concepts from this chapter can I work on, learn, or practice?

These concepts will increase the value of my family in what ways?

What can I do to apply these principles in a practical way?

Building Blocks for My Home

With concepts from this chapter, what are practical steps I can take to build my family and create a "healthier" home?

One:

Two:

Three:

Basic Blocks For Building

When facing trials:

1. Accept that trials, broken dreams, and tough times will come–it's not "if," rather, it's "when."
2. Accept that you cannot avoid tough times NOR prepare for specific tough times. Tough times just happen.
3. Be joyful regardless of the circumstances around you.
4. Be appreciative for what you have.
5. Be patient and learn from the tough times.
6. Realize that you cannot change the past–only the present and future.
7. Find healthy and constructive ways to remain positive.

When you find yourself in a tough time:

1. Evaluate your situation.
2. Hang on to your values and look for the silver lining.
3. Apply the lesson to a broader life and focus on the larger picture.
4. Re-evaluate where you spend and invest your time, money, life, daydreams, dreams, and energy.

Additional Suggested Resources:

Bennett, William J. *The De-Valuing of America.*
Dobson, James. *Love Must be Tough.*
Hart, Archibald D. *Children & Divorce.*
Minirth, Frank B. and Paul D. Meier. *Happiness Is a Choice.*
Tough Love International-contact them on line at: www.toughlove.org

Section Five

Protecting Your Investment

```
—Failure—

Climbing the ladder to success
only to discover it is leaning
against the wrong wall.
```

Chapter IX.
Insuring Your Home–Developing a
Successful Worldview

The single most important part of any structure is the foundation. I am often amazed at how long it takes for a tall building to begin to take shape. It seems like nothing is happening for months on end and then all at once, the steel structure is up. The builders know that if the foundation is flawed, it does not matter how sound the rest of the building is. What difference does it make if the walls, paint, trim, and marble works are perfect? If the foundation is faulty, the structure will not stand the test of the harsh elements over time.

Just like a tall building, a successful home must be built on a solid foundation. It is the best insurance against the storms that life often brings. In the second section, we discovered that the foundation for success is first and foremost success with self. But what is the key to success with self? A successful worldview is the key to success with self. You might be thinking, "What is a worldview?"

To put it simply, our worldview is the way we see the world. To put it another way, our worldview is the filter or lens through which we interpret the events and circumstances that impact our lives. You might ask,

"Why is worldview so important?" Our worldview determines our core values and philosophy of life. It determines the leadership of our life and thus the direction of the personal growth process described in Section Two. What is a successful worldview?

A successful worldview is one that correctly corresponds to the reality of the world we live in. Just imagine you are visiting Los Angeles and are trying to get from the Coliseum to Hollywood. You have a map that says City of Los Angeles, but due to a printing error, it is really a map of San Francisco. What would happen? Immediately you would be lost. You need a map that corresponds to the reality of your location–Los Angeles. In the same way, a successful banker must operate by sound banking principles or the resources of the investors are at risk. When constructing a bridge, structural engineers must understand all the forces at work and abide by the standards and codes or the lives of all who use the bridge are in danger. For a worldview to work, it must help us correctly navigate in the reality of planet earth.

To that end, a successful worldview must
correctly answer two key questions:
1) Is there a God?, and 2) If there is a God, who is it?

Is there a God?

To answer this question is to look at the issue of origins. Do we live in a world that can be explained correctly through natural causes—naturalism? Or do we live in a created world? Naturalism denies all supernatural involvement and asserts that nature is all that exists. For the naturalist this world and all of life came about by chance. You can see this idea in Carl Sagan's famous line from his television series, "The Cosmos is all that is, or ever was, or will ever be." If naturalism is true, the moral implications are staggering. If the world can be explained through natural causes, then this life is all there is. As humans we would then be no different from other animals having no intrinsic value. Truth would be a matter of preference with no such thing as right or wrong. What is right or moral would be up to the individual.

Science, which means "knowledge," is what we can see and know. It is what we can observe, test, and reproduce in a laboratory. Naturalism claims to be the scientific explanation for the origin of the Cosmos and for life on earth. The question every person must answer is: can naturalism answer these questions as measured by the scientific method or do we live in a created world? By the way, everyone involved in this debate agrees there are only two options, naturalism and creationism. Creationism cannot be measured by science since it claims to have happened in the

Can the universe and world we live in be explained by natural causes?

past, and therefore, cannot be observed or reproduced in a laboratory. If naturalism is true, through applying the rules of science we will be able to explain the origin of the universe and life on earth. We will be able to reproduce in a laboratory the origin of life from amino acids to the single cell. Then, observe its transformation to all of life as we know it today. If creation is true, science will reveal that while species have the ability to adapt, there has been no transformation from one species to another.

How did the Cosmos come into existence? Can the scientific method explain it? Naturalism points to the Big Bang as the beginning of the Cosmos. This, in itself, is an admission that there was a beginning. There was a time when the Cosmos was not. Remember, naturalism says, "The cosmos is all there is, or ever was, or ever will be." Even if the Big Bang Theory were true, it does not support naturalism. There are a growing number of creationists (proponents of the Intelligent Design Theory) who view the Big Bang as God's instrument in creating the universe. Isaac Newton, widely recognized as one of the greatest scientists who ever lived, came to the following conclusion on the complexities of the universe, "This most beautiful system of the sun, planets, and comets could only proceed from the counsel and dominion of an intelligent and powerful being."

Can naturalism, using the scientific method, explain the origin of life on this planet? Julian Huxley, one of the leading proponents of naturalism in the 20th century, defines evolution this way, "A directional and essentially irreversible process occurring in time, which in its course gives rise to an increase of variety and an increasingly high level of organization... in its products. Our present knowledge forces us to view that the whole of reality is evolution... a single process of self-transformation" (*What is Science?*, p.278). In short, naturalism would say that all life as we know it today rose through evolution and natural selection. Notice in this definition that it is occurring "in time," therefore, it should be observable.

Remember, science is what we can see and know. In all of human history no one has ever seen evolution take place. You might ask, what about the Peppered Moth in England? It changed from light to dark during the Industrial Revolution. As the trees turned dark due to the use of coal, the moth turned dark to blend in. However, now that England has been cleaned up it has adapted back to light. The Peppered Moth illustrates adaptation within species, not evolution. The simple fact is that the scientific method does not support naturalism. Evolution cannot be observed presently nor in the past through the fossil record.

Proponents of naturalism disagree and insist that past evolution is reflected in the fossil record. If evolution were true, the geological column would reflect ten geological ages in order, and it would be uniform around the world. The geological column would be filled with millions of transition fossils painting a clear portrait of the full development of life from amino acids to life as we know it today. In Darwin's time, the fossil record was the most serious objection to his theory. Darwin hoped that the rest of the picture would substantiate his theory. The opposite has happened. With over a quarter of a million fossil species, there is less support for his theory today than there was in his day. The geological column reflects a total absence of transition fossils. The examples that we all remember from our school textbooks (The Peppered Moth, Horses, Java Man, etc.) have been dismissed by naturalists themselves.

Naturalism cannot be observed in the present, the fossil record, nor can it be reproduced in the laboratory. Scientists have tried to reproduce the transition from the amino acids of the primeval soup to a single cell for more than forty years and have not even come close. Without this initial step (called spontaneous generation), the rest of the discussion is over. There are multiple inorganic chemical reactions that are scientifically impossible. Proponents of naturalism admit to this dilemma. Notice this statement from the late eighties, "More than thirty years of experimentation on the origin of life... have led to a better perception...

of the immensity of the problem of the origin of life on the earth, rather than to its solution" (Klaus Dose, *Interdisciplinary Science Reviews,* Vol 13, No. 4, 1988, p.348). Peter Franz agrees, "No one has ever produced a species by mechanism of natural selection. No one has ever gotten near it…" (Interview on BBC with Peter Franz, March 4, 1982). Two well-known scientists calculated the odds of life forming from natural processes at less than one in ten to the 40,000th. My naturalist friends respond to this argument ending roadblock with something like this: "In a million years anything impossible becomes probable, and anything probable becomes absolute scientific fact." This reflects "faith" in a worldview not the scientific method.

Again, science is "knowledge" that we know through observation and testing. Naturalism fails the test of science in explaining the origin of life. It is not being observed in the present, it is not seen in the past through the fossil record, and it has not been reproduced in a laboratory. Science points to a world full of species that have been the same throughout time. Many species, like the Peppered Moth, have adapted and thrived. Others, such as dinosaurs, were not able to adapt to environmental changes and became extinct. It is clear species have the ability to adapt, but not to transform from one to another.

Since naturalism cannot explain the origin of this world and the life it contains, we must, in fact, live in a created world. But who is the creator? Who is the God of this universe? And what does He want from us?

These questions and history demand that we ask and answer the question, who is Jesus Christ? Why? Jesus Christ has, without a doubt, impacted our world more than anyone else in history. He is a key figure in every world religion except Buddhism/Confucianism, which denies the reality of a personal God. For Muslims, Jesus was a great prophet; for Hindus, He was a great teacher; and finally Jesus claimed to be the promised Messiah for Judaism. Phillip Schaff, well-known historian and author, portrays well the impact of the life of Christ in the following statement; "Jesus of Nazareth, without money and arms, conquered more millions than Alexander, Caesar, Mohammed and Napoleon; without science and learning, He shed more light on human and divine issues than all philosophers and scholars combined; without the eloquence of the school, He spoke words of life such as were never spoken before, nor since, and produced effects which lie beyond the reach of orator or poet. Without writing a single line, He has set more pens in motion and furnished themes for more sermons, orations, discussions, works of art, learned volumes, and sweet songs of praise than the whole army of great men of ancient and modern times." Jesus Christ lived thirty-three short years and though He never published a book, led an army, nor had the benefit of the electronic media, His brief life literally split time. Every time we look at the date on a newspaper, a calendar, or write a check, we acknowledge the impact of His life.

Jesus Christ is different from other religious leaders in two critical points

Jesus Claimed to be God

Why is it that the names of the founders of other world religions never offend anyone? Have you ever thought about it? Names like Mohammed, Confucius, and Buddha? The answer is really quite simple. These men never claimed to be God! It didn't take long for the people who heard Jesus speak to realize that He was making some very incredible claims about Himself. Here are just a few:

HIS CLAIMS	REFERENCES
The Christ, the Son of God	Mark 14:61-64
Equality with God	John 10:31-38
I Am	John 8:58
Authority equal with God	John 8:19
The Way, The Truth, The Life	John 14:6
The Living Water	John 4:14
The Bread of Life	John 6:35, 51
The Good Shepherd	John 10:14-15
He received worship	Matthew 8:2; John 20:28

Theologian and scholar Herschel Hobbs writes of how Jesus made even His trial leaders admit to His claims. Here's how: When they asked Jesus, "Art thou then the Son of God?" Jesus answered, "Ye say that I am." By answering their question in that manner, He forced them to admit to His deity. Therefore, they sentenced Him to death not only by His own testimony, which they considered blasphemous, but by their own as well.

Jesus most assuredly claimed to be more than just a prophet or a great teacher. He was obviously making claims to deity... He claimed to be God! He said that He and He alone is the only avenue to a right relationship with God. In other words, He said that without Him in your life, you cannot truly and intimately know God. Jesus made it clear that a meaningful, purposeful life, without frustration, guilt, or loneliness is found only in Him.

The claims of Jesus Christ back us into the corner of decision. We must go one way or the other when we carefully consider what He said. He left no other option. I often hear people say, "I'm ready to accept Jesus as a great moral teacher, but I'm not ready to accept His claim to be God." They allow that Jesus was a great moral teacher. However, if that is their real belief, rejecting Jesus' claims to be God would make Him either a lunatic or a liar.

C. S. Lewis, once an agnostic and a professor at Cambridge University, understood this position quite clearly. In fact when he came to that inevitable fork in the road he committed his life to Christ and became one of the greatest writers and defenders of the faith. C. S. Lewis' inescapable conclusions expressed in his book, *Mere Christianity*, have been taught the world over. **He concluded that Jesus is either a liar, a lunatic, or the Lord.**

If we reject Jesus' claim to be God, then we have only two alternatives. Jesus either knew He was not God and lied, or He thought He was God and thus fell into the ranks of one of history's greatest lunatics. In fact, He would be the chief lunatic. First...

Was Jesus a Liar?

Almost everyone will admit to the fact that Jesus was a great moral teacher. How could He be a great moral teacher and mislead literally millions of people at the most important point of His teaching...His own identity? If He were moral, He couldn't do that! When He said, *"I am the Way, the Truth, and the Life,"* (John 14:6)... or *"I am the Bread of Life,"* (John 6:35) or *"I am the Good Shepherd,"* (John 10:11) and knew that He wasn't all of these things, then it is logical to conclude that He was a deliberate liar, that He conceived, planned, and carried out the world's greatest hoax.

This view of Jesus, however, does not coincide with what we know about Him and the results of His life and work. It just doesn't make sense in the face of the countless people whose lives were changed through His ministry and since because of His teachings.

A good example of the powerful impact that Jesus Christ can have on a life is recorded in the memoirs of the great French General Napoleon. Here's what he said about Jesus, "I know men: and I tell you that Jesus Christ is not a man. Superficial minds see a resemblance between Christ and the founders of empires, and the gods of other religions. That resemblance does not exist. The distance of infinity is between Christianity and whatever other religions there are. Everything in Christ astonishes me. His Spirit overawes me, and His will confounds me. I search in vain in history to find anyone similar to Christ, or anything that can approach the beauty of the gospel. Neither history, nor humanity, nor the ages, nor nature, offer me anything with which I am able to compare it or to explain it. Here everything is extraordinary." (Grounds, Vernon C. *The Reason for Our Hope*. Chicago: Moody Press, 1945. p.37).

Napoleon was right! Wherever Jesus has been proclaimed, lives have been changed for the good. Nations have been built for the better.

> ## *HE just keeps on changing lives.*

Thieves have been made honest. Alcoholics and drug addicts have been cured and reformed. Hateful individuals have become channels of love. Prostitutes have been forgiven and made whole again. Unjust persons have become just... and on and on. He just keeps on changing lives!

The great historian Philip Schaff makes this comment: "A character so original, so complete, so uniformly consistent, so perfect, so human and yet so high above human greatness, can be neither a fraud nor a fiction... it would take more than a Jesus to invent a Jesus." (Schaff, Philip. *History of the Christian Church*. 8 vols. Grand Rapids: Wm. B. Eerdmands Publishing Co. 1910, reprint from original, 1962. p.109).

As you ponder the alternatives, please be wise enough to realize that it would have been totally impossible for Jesus to have lived, taught and died the way He did and be a liar.

Was Jesus a Lunatic?

Is it possible that Jesus could have thought Himself to be God, and simply been mistaken? After all, it is possible for someone to be sincere, yet sincerely wrong… sound familiar? For someone to claim to be God, especially in the monotheistic (belief in one God) culture into which He was born, borders on insanity. To go further, for someone to make such claims and then to tell others that their eternal destiny, meaning, purpose, and identity depended upon their believing in Him, would be the thoughts of a lunatic such as the world has not often seen — not my idea of a sincere misconception about oneself.

Was Jesus Christ such a madman? Was Jesus so mentally deranged as to have been able to dream up such a hoax? When we study His life, these types of abnormalities and imbalances do not exist, not only from what is recorded in the Bible, but in other innumerable writings. In fact, just the opposite emerges. His poise and composure would certainly be incredible if He were insane.

Psychiatrist J. T. Fisher, quoted in Josh McDowell's best selling book, *More Than a Carpenter*, said, "If you were to take the sum total of all authoritative articles ever written by the most qualified of psychologists and psychiatrists on the subject of mental hygiene, and were to combine them and redefine them so as to cleave out the excess verbiage, then, if you were to have these unadulterated bits of pure scientific knowledge concisely expressed by the most capable of living poets, you would have an awkward and incomplete summation of the Sermon on the Mount. For 2,000 years the Christian world has been holding in its hand the complete answer to its restless and fruitless yearnings. Here rests the blueprint for successful human life with optimism, mental health, and contentment."

I heartily agree with Even Channing, who said, "The charge of an extravagant, self-deluding enthusiasm is the last to be fastened on Jesus Christ." (Schaff, Philip. *The Person of Christ*. New York, American Tract Society, 1913, p.98).

How could anyone hang on Jesus of Nazareth, whose life and teachings impacted the world like no other, the tag of a lunatic? This is one you shouldn't have to do much thinking on.

The claims of Christ back us right into the corner of decision. You cannot dismiss Him as a great prophet or recognize Him as a great moral teacher. Those are not valid options. He is either a liar, a lunatic, or the Lord. You must make the choice. The evidence is overwhelming that Jesus is Lord!

> *There are risks and costs to a program of action, but they are far less than the long-range risks and costs of comfortable inaction.*
> *—John F. Kennedy*

So far, we have said that Jesus was different from the founders and leaders of the world's other religions in that, first, He claimed to be God and none of the others did. Second, He sealed His claim forever in history with His resurrection.

Jesus Arose from the Grave

Speaking of the resurrection, how can we be sure of any historical data or facts? Most historians define a historical fact as "knowledge of the past based upon reliable testimony."

For example, is there anyone you know who has ever seen any of the Caesars of Rome? We rely upon the testimonies of others passed through time to know anything at all about them. However, I have never met anyone that denies their existence.

The resurrection of Christ rests upon the same type of testimonies, but is in actuality more reliable due to the facts that surround the eyewitness accounts. I John 1:1-3, and Acts 1:1-3 relate some of the testimonies; however, II Peter 1:16 specifically states, *"For we did not follow cleverly devised tales when we made known to you the power and coming of our Lord Jesus Christ, but we were eyewitnesses of His majesty."*

The apostles' testimonies can be trusted because of two critical points. Ten of the original eleven died martyrs' deaths because of their witness to the resurrection and their belief in Him as the Son of God. These men were beaten, stoned, flogged, and crucified upside down. Each faced death by some of the cruelest methods known to man. Examples include:

Peter........... crucified	Simon...................crucified
Andrew.......crucified	Thaddaeus.....killed by arrows
Matthew.........sword	James.......................stoned
James.........crucified	Thomas..............spear thrust
Philip.........crucified	Bartholomew..........crucified

John......normal death (received the Revelation while in exile)

I have heard many respond something like this: "Big deal, others have died for a lie. What does that prove?" True, others have died for a lie, but here is the difference: They thought it was the truth. Now, if the resurrection didn't take place, the disciples would have been the first to know it. They would have not only known it was a lie, they would have been the ones to have conceived the hoax.

The argument that these witnesses of Christ's life, death, and resurrection all lied about it and were killed with the same lie on their lips does not make sense! Some, like Peter, were men of wealth. First, what did they have to gain? They experienced only pain, sorrow, trials, rejection, poverty, and untimely death. Christ's followers would not have faced poverty, torture and death unless they were absolutely convinced of the resurrection. They WERE convinced! How were they convinced? They saw it! But remember, Jesus said the ones who believed without having seen would be more blessed. That's you and me!

Second, the disciples' mind-set at the time of the crucifixion was one of great fear and confusion until they saw Him resurrected and alive. History records that it was only after the resurrection that they understood the reason for Christ's death on the cross and the hope of the resurrection. Dr. Simon Greenleaf, while a professor of the Harvard School of Law evaluated the legal nature of their testimony and wrote, "... They knew His resurrection life was a fact as certainly as they knew any other fact."

We can also be most assured of the reality of our Lord's resurrection as we look at the changed lives of His followers, namely Peter.

The life of Peter provides incredible and undeniable proof of the resurrection. As one studies the historical records, every time Peter is found standing next to Jesus, he was always very courageous. During the Last Supper, he is the only one who said emphatically that he would never deny the Lord. Peter, in reality, said that he would die first.

Jesus predicted that he would deny Him. Nevertheless, Peter was always brave, or should we say impulsive, when it came to what he was going to do for Jesus. Oh yes, he was very strong—when Jesus was around.

Remember the story of how he cut off the ear of a guard when Jesus was being arrested in the Garden of Gethsemane! Strong! Brave! Tough! (At least when Jesus was around.) Peter would have attempted almost anything if he thought Jesus would have been there to back him up! He was overly courageous with the Master by his side.

However, without Jesus around he was 'spineless'. After the arrest of the Lord, Peter was standing by a fire and was literally backed down by a teenage girl who recognized him. He was full of fear and intimidated by an adolescent without Jesus. Strange! He would take on the entire Roman army with Jesus at his side, but without Jesus, he was weak. Peter couldn't even stand for Him before one teenage girl.

Now the question is, how could this man who was so beset by fear and insecurity without Jesus by his side, stand on the day of Pentecost in the presence of the ones who actually killed Jesus and preach a ten minute message calling them the murderers of the Lord of glory? The answer is simple: The resurrected, living Lord Jesus was alive within Peter.

There were at least ten recorded post-resurrection appearances, including Christ's overwhelming revelation to the apostle Paul that drastically changed his life. In fact, one of the great questions of history is: What happened to Paul? One day he was persecuting, murdering, and arresting Christians by the thousands. Then, he suddenly changed into one of the most powerful voices for God who has ever lived. How did this happen? What changed Paul so drastically? The same thing that happened to Peter! He saw the risen, reigning Christ and was transformed immediately when Jesus came to live inside of him.

Then, there are the facts that surround the empty tomb. For example, listen to just a few steps that were taken to keep Jesus in the tomb. You see, even though the very ones who crucified Him denied His claims as the Son of God, they still wanted the tomb guarded in order to prevent fulfillment of His prophecy of coming back from the dead (Matthew 27:57-66).

◆ Jesus was placed in a new tomb that was carved out of the side of a rocky ledge. The stone that covered the tomb weighed over two tons and was placed in a slanted downhill groove.

◆ The huge stone had what is called the "Roman Grave Seal" that stretched from one side to the other and was placed into wax in order that the guards could see with a glance if anyone were to tamper with the tomb.

◆ There were sixteen of the best guards that this particular garrison of the Roman Empire had to offer. It was an around the clock job they were given, with the loss of their life in case someone passed them by and stole the body of Christ. Each soldier had a six-foot territory to cover with a back up.

There are several theories of what happened to the body of Jesus. By the way, theories themselves indicate that something did happen. However, for the sake of time we will only look at three.

First, there is the "Roman and/or Jewish authorities stolen body theory." If this is true, why didn't they produce the body and kill the so-called Christian hope in a moment? They couldn't produce it, because they didn't steal it.

Second, there is the "disciples and friends stolen body theory." The testimony of the disciples was discussed earlier. They wouldn't have died for a lie. Additionally, they would have had to come up with an idea or a plan to break through all of the security above–likely not possible for the disciples and friends.

Third, there is the "Swoon theory." This theory claims that Jesus was not totally dead, and the dampness of the empty tomb revived Him, so He pushed away the stone, slipped past the guards, and returned home. In the first place, the Romans were experts at putting people to death. They checked the body of Jesus twice, but the real evidence of death was when the spear was thrust into the side and blood and water gushed out. This combination proved Jesus was dead.

There are other theories, such as the wild animal theory, which says that animals got into the tomb and dragged the body off, or the wrong tomb theory, which states that Jesus was buried in the wrong place. Honestly, the miracle of the resurrection is much more plausible than any of these theories.

Science clearly reveals that we live in a created world. History points to the fact that Jesus has impacted our world more than any one who has ever lived. Additionally, history points to the truth that He claimed to be God, and sealed His claim with His resurrection. The only logical conclusion is that He certainly is not a liar, nor is He a lunatic, rather, He is the Lord. Therefore, the worldview that fits the reality of the world in which we live is the Christian worldview. What then does God want from us? God wants a relationship with us. In fact, He wants one so badly that He sent Jesus to earth to die on a cross that through His death and resurrection we might find forgiveness and an eternal relationship with Him.

The life of Leo Tolstoy perfectly illustrates the truth of this chapter. He rejected Christianity as a child as he began his search for the meaning of life. First, he looked to pleasure entering the social world of Moscow and St. Petersburg drinking heavily and having many different sexual relationships. Pleasure simply did not satisfy him. Next, he tried wealth. Tolstoy had inherited an estate and was wealthy, but then he made a lot of money off his books. Again, wealth did not satisfy him.

He then decided fame and success must be the key. Tolstoy wrote *War and Peace*, which Encyclopedia Britannica described as one of the two or three greatest novels in world literature–again, he found that it did not satisfy him. Finally, he tried family. He had married in 1862 and had a happy family with thirteen children which probably distracted him from any search for the overall meaning of life.

He had achieved all his goals and was surrounded by what is considered to be complete happiness. Yet, one question brought him to the verge of suicide: **"What meaning has my life that the inevitability of death does not destroy?"**

Eventually he found, in the peasant people of Russia, a faith in Jesus Christ. Leo Tolstoy found in the Christian worldview he had rejected as a young child, what he had been searching for all his life. Tolstoy spent most of his life climbing the ladder to success, only to find that it was leaning against the wrong wall. It was a personal relationship with Jesus

Christ that brought meaning and purpose to his life.

To use a tennis metaphor, the ball is in your court. If I am right, the Christian worldview is the map that represents the reality of the world we live in. Just as you can't navigate in Los Angeles with a map of San Francisco, you can't deal with the realities of this world without a relationship with the God Who created it. This means that you, like Tolstoy, will never find what you're looking for in your life and family apart from a personal relationship with Christ. However, only you can make that decision. It is my sincere prayer and hope that if you do not know Christ you will begin an exciting and fulfilling relationship with Him. If you already have a relationship with Christ my prayer is that you will spend the rest of your life growing to your maximum potential in Him. Regardless, it has been an honor discussing with you how to build a successful family. May these basic building blocks help you discover your purpose as a family, grow to your maximum potential, and beginning in the home, sow seeds that benefit others. If you're interested in beginning a relationship with Jesus Christ, keep reading and you will discover just how to get started.

When you think about it, the Bible only teaches four simple things:
1. God loves us and has an incredible plan for our lives.
From the Garden of Eden to John 10:10 where Jesus said, "I have come that you might have life and have it abundantly," God makes it clear that He wants us to be in relationship with Him.
2. We have rejected God's incredible offer of abundant life.
God loves us so much that He does not demand that we accept His plan…He lets us choose. The Bible says in Romans 3:23 that, "All have sinned and fallen short of the glory of God." Romans 6:23 states, "That the wages of sin is death," Which means separation from God. Our lives and world are messed up because of our rebellion against God and His plan.
3. God has a cure for our sin problem.
Jesus came to the earth and lived the perfect life we could not live and then died on the cross to pay for our sin. Romans 5:8 says, "God showed His love for us in that while we were yet sinners, Christ died for us." Imagine that we are on one side of the Grand Canyon and

God is on the other. The chasm represents our sin. The cross is the bridge.

4. We must respond to God's offer of a relationship through Christ. We must cross the bridge. It takes three things:

♦ **We must admit that we need God**—"For by grace you are saved by faith, and that not of yourselves, it is a gift of God."

♦ **We must be willing to turn from our sin**—"Repent therefore, and turn again, that your sins may be blotted out, and that times of refreshing may come from the presence of the Lord."

♦ **We must ask Christ to come into our lives to be our Lord and Savior**—"If you confess with your mouth Jesus is Lord and believe in your heart that God has raised Him from the dead you will be saved...everyone who calls on the name of the Lord will be saved."

The following prayer expresses the above scriptural requirements. If this prayer expresses the desire of your heart and you pray it to God, (don't be nervous—prayer is just talking to God), Christ will come into your life and you will begin a new and exciting relationship with God. You will be immediately forgiven and will receive the gift of eternal life.

> Dear Lord Jesus, I admit that I've
> sinned and need forgiveness.
> I ask You to come into my heart,
> forgive my sin, take control of my life,
> and help me be all that You made me to be.
> I believe You are the Son of God
> and that You died for me and rose again.
> Thank You for coming into my heart
> to be my Lord and Savior.

If you have prayed this prayer, or prayed a similar prayer in your own words committing your life to Jesus, you have received the free gift of eternal life and have begun a new and exciting relationship with God.

How to be sure that you have a relationship with God and have received the free gift of eternal life:

♦ **You can trust God's promise**—"Everyone who calls on the name of the Lord will be saved" (Romans 10:13). Did you sincerely ask Jesus into your heart as Lord and Savior? Where is He right now? What does God's Word promise?

♦ **You are eternally secure in God's love**—"For I am convinced that neither death nor life, neither angels nor demons, neither the present nor the future, nor any powers, neither height nor depth, nor anything else in all creation, will be able to separate us from the love of God that is in Christ Jesus our Lord" (Romans 8:38-39).

Welcome to God's family!

You have just begun the most rewarding and fulfilling relationship in all of life. To develop your new relationship with Christ you should:

♦ Communicate with God daily by reading the Bible and talking with Him through prayer.

♦ Worship, fellowship, and serve Him through a local church where Christ is preached and the Bible is clearly taught.

♦ Be sensitive to those around you and look for opportunities to meet needs and share what you have found in Christ.

Additional Suggested Resources:

Colson, Charles and Nancy Pearcey. *How Now Shall We Live?*
Institute of Creation Research—contact them on line at: www.icr.org
Johnson, Phillip E. *Darwin on Trial.*
Johnson, Phillip E. *The Wedge of Truth.*
Lewis, C. S. *Mere Christianity.*
McDowell, Josh. *More Than a Carpenter.*
McDowell, Josh. *Evidence That Demands a Verdict.*

To order additional copies of this book or
for information on bringing a
Building a Successful Family Conference
to your city or organization,
please call or write:

1-770-995-8686

Jerry Pipes Productions
P.O. Box 490338
Lawrenceville, Georgia 30049